M000237664

The Dating Mirror

Trust Again, Love Again

By Diana Dorell and Maryellen Smith

Copyright © 2015 Diana Dorell and Maryellen Smith

All rights reserved. No part of this book may be reproduced or transmitted in any form or by any means without written permission of the publisher, except in the case of brief quotations embodied in critical articles and reviews.

This material had been written and published solely for educational purposes. The author and the publisher shall have neither liability nor responsibility to any person or entity with respect to any loss, damage, or injury caused or alleged to be caused directly or indirectly by the information contained in this book.

The author of this book does not dispense medical advice or prescribe the use of any technique as a form of treatment for physical, emotional, or medical problems without the advice of a physician, either directly or indirectly. The intent of the author is only to offer information of a general nature to help you in your quest for wellbeing. In the event you use any of the information in this book for yourself or others, which is your constitutional right, the author and the publisher assume no responsibility for your actions.

Statements made in this book have not been evaluated by the Food and Drug Administration. This book and its contents are not intended to diagnose, treat, or cure any infection, injury, or illness, or prevent any disease. Results vary and each person's experience is unique.

ISBN: 978-0-9884471-7-2

Babypie Publishing
Waitsfield, VT
www.BabypiePublishing.com

Praise for The Dating Mirror

"Maryellen and Diana are the perfect combination of big sister-meets best girlfriend-meets I don't-take-any-crap coaches that will call you out on yourself every single time. This book has a lot of wisdom in it. I'd recommend it to help you improve any of your relationships, not just romantic ones. LOVED it!"

— Alicia Orre, Business Marketing Coach
AliciaOrre.com

"From how to read a potential date from just their online profile and photos to establishing a contract with yourself on your personal love needs and boundaries, this book covers it all — intuition, relationship red-flags, dates from Hell and practical steps towards finding your own match made in Heaven. Love is work. But Diana and Maryellen have given us the tools to make it a heck of a lot of fun — with plenty of personalized questionnaires and step-by-step methods on how to navigate today's world of romance armed with our most powerful ally — intuition — to help us re-discover the most potent potion of them all: self-love."

— Neil D. Paris, author
Surfing Your Solar Cycles: A Lifetime Guide to Your Stars
newworldastrology.com

"This is an intelligent, practical, fun and funny how-to guide through the maze and minefield, not just of the landscape and best practices of dating, but of finding our best mate by developing and appreciating our talents and abilities. When we realize the importance of qualifying partners for what we want and deserve, vs. just hoping and working to be picked, then we are our strongest and most true, and are most attractive to our ideal mate."

— Jennifer Rosenwald, #1 international bestselling author
The Expert Success Solution
Speaker, Trainer, Business & Personal Coach
jenniferrosenwald.com

"I am so grateful to Diana and Maryellen for writing this book. I'd recommend it to anyone who is interested in having great relationships or for Moms to read to help their daughters navigate the tough dating landscape. It's chock-full of real, practical advice from real life stories that are eye-opening and fun to read."
— Sasha Niala, Integrative Healer and Artist
Sashaniala.com

"I have three words for You: *give me more*! This book is a breath of fresh air to the dating perspective. These ladies blend their intuitiveness and experience with the dating insight. Ladies, we are in this together — this is a must read! Continued love and blessings, Goddesses Diana and Maryellen!
— Maria San Juan, The Healing Diva
thehealingdiva.com

"This book is life changing. I know that sounds so cheesy, but seriously, for anyone who has struggled with confidence in dating, go buy this for yourself and all your girlfriends! I've stopped feeling embarrassed or shy about what I really want and for once, I can say with confidence, I am a great catch and I deserve love. Thanks ladies!"
— Carenda Rudis

"Before I read this book, it seemed like I would get have the same relationship problems over and over. Different guy, same situation. Now I understand how to use my intuition and see red flags early."
— Zack Hall

"Before I read this book, I felt like there was something wrong with me. Now I know that intuition is a natural thing and when we listen to it, things feel easy and we aren't crazy after all! What a relief! It definitely grabbed my attention!"
— Andrea Pérez, Intuitive Life Coach

"I LOVED this book! It is a real game-changer. There are other dating books out there that hint at intuition in dating but they don't go into detail about how to tap into your sixth sense."
— Mindy Crary, owner of Creative Money
creativemoney.biz
Author
Personal Finance that Doesn't Suck

"Buy this book for yourself and get a copy for all your girlfriends. While you're at it, don't forget your LGBT friends too! We can all benefit. It has awesome, practical dating advice that will help you become a stronger, sexier version of yourself. And who doesn't want to be a confident love magnet?"

—RD Riccoboni, World-Renowned Artist
www.rdriccoboni.com

"Dating, whether in real life or online, is tricky business. This book breaks the codes, and there are many of them, to help you navigate all the signs available in an online profile, and in face-to-face interactions. Too often we do not recognize or turn away from early warning signs that can keep us from going down a unpleasant dating rabbit hole. Then along comes a refreshing, honest, intelligent, and—most importantly—strategic dating guide book. Whether you are new to online dating or finding incomplete success (getting dates, but not a lasting relationship), this book is a must read before you forge ahead or back into the world of online dating. Use it as you would your brakes and seat belt in your car when you see cautionary signs or need to make an abrupt stop before going over a cliff. At their best, these authors teach you to be in integrity with yourself, which, in turn, will help you see the profiles of people of equal integrity so you can have a positive dating experience and find both the relationship you want and the one you deserve."

—Philip Young, PhD
Black Unykorn Tarot and Astrology
www.blackunykorn.com

"I am so happy someone has finally written this book! It is incredibly practical and user friendly, particularly for the intuitively inclined. I'm excited to finally have a reliable resource to recommend to my coaching clients who are looking to attract their perfect partner!"
—Lauren L'Amour, Life Visionary
lifevisionary.com

"Reading this book was like sitting down with your two best girlfriends who tell it like it is over a cup of coffee, drawing on their own experiences as examples of how to navigate the dating world."

—Lisa D.

"My online dating experience was only a four-month journey,

but long enough to say that Maryellen and Diana have hit the nail on the head with this one! Several times I didn't even meet the person after a "gut feeling" I had after a brief phone conversation, and the longest lasted fewer than ninety days when after forgiving one lie caught him in another. Lying is definitely a deal-breaker! I did meet "Mr. Right" online, and followed the very practical advice in this book! Thank you both for your fine work. Many women won't have to learn the hard way!"

— Kim M.

"Okay, ladies, RUN — don't walk — to get this book! Seriously, if you're single and you are tired of feeling crazy and alone, Diana and Maryellen will set you straight and give you super simple tips that actually WORK. Go get it!"

— Kathi Casey
The Healthy Boomer Body Expert
fitwomenboomers.com

"I'd highly recommend this book to intuitive women who are tired of feeling drained from dating. Before I read this book, I would not understand why my dates didn't work out. I would be so optimistic and then be so disappointed afterwards. Now I understand how to interpret my intuition and have more realistic expectations. Thank you ladies for putting this amazing information together!"

— Lynn "Louie" Bischoff

"This book illuminates intuition, which is as fundamental to life as being made of water or breathing air. When you access your intuition all of your life experiences will flow with more grace and ease."

— Patrick Durkin, Founder
GodSelf University, www.godself.com

Acknowledgements

From Diana:

I'll never forget the day that Maryellen and I both blurted out the words, "Let's write a book!" over chai lattes. I don't know if it was the caffeine rush, excitement, fate or a combo of all of those, but the air was electric and once we started, we were on a roll, adding to the idea one sentence after another until we were laughing like loonies in the coffee shop.

"Yes!" It'll be a book about dating and all the highs, lows and unmistakably powerful lessons we've both been through in the past year. Or wait, correction: I mean for the past *decade*. Between you and me there's gotta be enough for two books!"

Even though the mood that day was light, I knew in my core it was going to happen. *When?* I had no idea. Like most of the miraculous things I've experienced in my life, I'd learned that the how and when are really out of our control. Spirit really does things on its own time. And with a sense of humor. Nothing is ever what we expect!

It can be so much better.

That's the intuitive path—getting out of your own way and trusting that you'll be shown all you need along the path. Throughout the entire process of this book's birth, I have been a faithful student.

I want to acknowledge first and foremost my Bombshell goddess partner-in-crime, Maryellen Smith, for so much more than I'm able to fully express on the page.

Maryellen, thank you so much for believing in this book and its message every step of the way. For keeping us in line in your amazing Virgo fashion and reigning me in when I started to go off on one of my crazy Leo creative tangents! And for being such a true, patient and amazing friend.

I love you. Thank you. We did it, Bombshell. We *did* it!

I also want to acknowledge my parents, my sister Susan, my family in Arizona and Venezuela, and my Soul sisters Carenda Rudis, Patty Rose, Helen Mears, Natalie Vartanian, Sally Hope, Priscilla Stephan. You have all been so supportive and encouraging, helping me stay the course and hold true to my vision always.

To Spirit and my Angels, for guiding us every step of the way.

So many more people to thank for support, inspiration and wisdom: Keith Leon, without you and your talented team, we would not be holding this book in our hands. Michelle Eld for your initial edits. Marie Forleo, Katherine Woodward Thomas, Colette Baron-Reid, Sonia Choquette, Althea Gray and Doreen Virtue.

And finally, to all the single Goddesses out there: believe in love, always.

From Maryellen:

Anyone who has ever written a book knows that it is a process; a process that involves many people. There is not only the writing, but the editing and publishing — to make something that was a dream become a physical reality. Then, there are all the people who contributed to the experiences in the book. Whether those experiences are good or bad, the interaction was significant enough to be shared for a life lesson or a maybe even a quick laugh. To all my life teachers, I am grateful.

Above anyone else, I'd like to thank my friend and collaborator Diana Dorell for being unflinchingly dedicated to getting this information out into the world. From the first time that I met Diana in 2009, I was impressed by her willingness to reveal her raw, uncensored human side for the purpose of allowing others to see themselves and to heal. Thank you Diana. Namaste.

I'm dedicating this book to my family. To my mother who always told me that I could do anything that I wanted to do without introducing any doubt into that belief. To my father from whom I inherited my creative entrepreneurial spirit. To my brother Charlie who has been my steadfast life-long supporter. To my brother Tommy who has helped me become the person that I am today simply by being himself.

Thank you also to Will Bachand for being the most loving and supportive life partner that I could imagine.

Last but not least, thank you to Keith Leon from Babypie Publishing for helping us get this work into physical form. Diana and I appreciate you much more than you could ever imagine.

Table of Contents

Foreword

What exactly is intuition? Intuition is a messaging system that comes from your inner source of knowing. You can feel strongly, *know*, that something is true but you don't necessarily have proof or evidence of it. The fact that you don't have proof doesn't diminish the truth of what you know.

I started The Center for Intuitive Development in 1996 as an educational center for personal and professional development and spiritual growth. We work with thousands of men, women and families each year. I can tell you with 100 percent confidence that learning to listen to and use your internal guidance system is the path to living an authentic, purpose-driven life. You might not even know what that means, listening to your inner guidance, but I assure you, you can learn.

Conscious interactions are at the core of successful relationships. When you think about it, you have all kinds of relationships. You have relationships to your biological family, you have relationships with friends, you have a relationship with food, you have a relationship with money and you have romantic relationships, to name a few. Those relationships can be healthy, conscious and aware or they can be mindless and automatic.

Think about going on a diet. Going on a diet is about consciously reconnecting with food healthily. You probably already know what healthy food is. The challenge is not all about what you eat, but about eating consciously. When you eat consciously you know what's good for you and what isn't.

When it comes to relationships, you might not think you can be as conscious of what's good for you as you can with food. But, you can! It's all about re-training yourself to know who you are at your core. This does not mean that you are going to have to spend the rest of your life alone. This is about being authentic, genuine and empowered. This is about nurturing your inner guidance and becoming the strongest, best version of yourself. Nobody is better at being you than you are, so you might as well become an expert at it. As you come into greater alignment with who you really are, you cultivate and attract relationships that mirror this.

At The Center for Intuitive Development we focus on embracing challenges and help you understand what supports you and how to be accountable. When you learn how to focus on these areas, you'll live a more empowered life. At the end of the day, that's what we all really want, even though we might go about it differently. Everyone wants a life of passion, purpose and peace. And in order to have those things, trusting your intuition and learning how to be authentic are essential. It's where everything else comes from.

This book you hold in your hands was written by two of my students in the spirit of learning how to be authentic in romantic relationships. I might not say things the exact same way as they do. However, we all have the same goal; to teach people how to check in with the internal compass that we all have. They have outlined core spiritual principles that you can use to help you identify and trust your intuition in any situation that life throws at you. To illustrate these principles, they have shared candid, entertaining stories to help you see firsthand how your intuition can guide you when you feel lost in the dark when it comes to dating.

If this is your introduction to the world of intuition, don't worry, you are in good hands! Some of what you may find in these pages may surprise you or ask you to look at yourself in a way you haven't before. But like any great relationship, it all starts with a strong foundation, a willingness to be vulnerable and the courage to dive into new territory with an open heart and mind. I wish you unlimited passion, purpose and peace! Reading this book is the great first step towards that.

Enjoy the journey!

Lynn M. Bunch

Founder of The Center for Intuitive Development

intuitivedevelopment.org

Beauty is eternity gazing at itself in a mirror. But you are eternity and you are the mirror.
— Kahil Gibran

Introduction

Your head has a lot of questions. Your heart has all your answers. No matter how much you justify something in your head, you're never going to make your heart believe something that you know isn't true. And there's no other area in which this plays out as much as in dating.

One of the benefits of having good girlfriends is that when you talk to them, you can listen to yourself. In the process of listening to yourself, you can hear things in a new way, a way that gives you insights into your thoughts, feelings and behavior. You'll be going on and on about some hot guy you met and how you think it's going to work out. Then, you see *the look* from your BFF. You know *the look,* it's the one where she's determining whether she's a better friend if she goes along with your excitement or if she keeps her mouth shut. It's the unspoken code of girlfriend honor that if she doesn't burst your bubble right now, with a right-between-the-eyes question, you won't do that to her the next time she's in the hot-new-guy bubble. Enough already! Be willing to see what is in front of you and don't be afraid to tell her what you see. If you can't do that, call your best gay guy friend. He will tell it like it is!

We wrote this book because we were tired of learning dating lessons in retrospect. That is truly the hard way! Even though we are from very different backgrounds, have a lot of years between us and are at different places in life, our dating situations were suspiciously similar. This isn't the same old dating BS about the differences between men and women and how they think. This is about being an intuitive woman and understanding how we're tuning out our intuition when it comes to dating. In most areas of our lives, we're honoring our intuitive gifts, our innate knowing and goddess energy. However, when it comes to dating, we're turning the volume down on our intuition, or worse yet, turning it OFF! Then we're confused when relationships don't work out.

What is this book about? The book is about honoring yourself, who you are and the person you intend to become. It's about breaking out of the dating/relationship pattern that keeps you stuck, once and for all. It's about loving yourself, creating a supportive community and being 100 percent totally okay with who you are in the world. Now, that is damn sexy! There is nothing like confidence to attract a man. The thing is, you've got to learn how to be discriminating and we'll show you how to tap into what you already know. Even if you don't follow our advice but have an *awareness* of your dating intuition, you'll be better off than you have been in the past.

Kierkegaard was only half correct when he said: "Life can only be understood backwards, but it must be lived forwards." We do have to live life forward but we don't have to have had an experience in the past to understand it in the present. Have you ever thought: I know I shouldn't <u>insert just about anything here</u>? Something probably popped into your head when you ignored your intuition and thought back on it later. *I knew I shouldn't have done that!* Those same big clues are right in front of you when it comes to dating; you just need to know how to change your view of the situation.

What this book is NOT about: acceptance of your life without a mate. We love and adore men and think they add huge value and pleasure to our lives. What this book IS about: tuning into your perceptions so that you can date with your eyes wide open. If you're like us, you've probably gotten pretty good at tuning out some very obvious signals. *How did I not see that coming? Same guy, different package? Really, Universe? I thought I learned that lesson already!*

This book is about learning to see more clearly so that your dating and relationship experiences aren't devastating. You won't be in a position where you've been blindsided and didn't see bad stuff coming.

Maybe that seems unromantic, to know an outcome before a relationship is fully evolved. Here's the deal…if you're intuitive and you're going into dating relationships blindly, there is a huge energetic cost to you. Without realizing it, you may be compromising your health, prosperity and longevity. Every area of your life affects the other. You can't dishonor yourself in a relationship without creating some imbalance in other areas. Yes, life has stress and challenges that you have to work through, but you have to be aligned at your core with your dating partners. There has to be a knowledge that certain fundamental aspects are in order with who you are. Going to a French restaurant if you don't like French food but your mate does is a circumstantial compromise, and that is fine. Your guy being a devout Catholic and you being spiritual but not religious is probably not going to work. This of course is a more obvious energetic difference than we're talking about, but you get the point.

Read on and see what we're talking about. Get ready to take a journey where you will see your dating challenges in a new, clearer way. Give yourself the gift of living and understanding life forward. Be willing to boost your energy and confidence in a new and exciting way from which you will never turn back.

This book is organized into easy-to-read chapters that include stories from each of us and from friends and clients. You can read one chapter after another or read individual chapters again and again. You'll pick up something different from each reading.

At the beginning of each chapter, we've outlined what

you'll learn from that section. We did this so that you could focus on the areas that are most meaningful for you or that you think would be helpful to share with a friend. Now, what are you waiting for? Turn the page!

Chapter 1
Are You an Intuitive Woman?

I feel there are two people inside me: me and my intuition. If I go against her, she'll screw me every time, and if I follow her, we get along quite nicely.
— Kim Basinger

Has the phone ever rung and you knew exactly who was calling? Do your friends ask your advice because you always understand? Do you sometimes feel drained or tired around certain people and don't know why?

An intuitive woman is someone who is most likely the go-to person in a crisis. She's the person you call when you need to feel better about your life. She knows how a situation is going to play out before it happens and has a strange knack for always being right. There are certain ways that we can access our intuition. Depending on which way is dominant, there are certain questions and tips you can implement to give you even deeper access into yourself and ultimately, the people you choose to date.

By the end of this chapter you will:

- Identify the characteristics of an intuitive woman
- Know the dominant channels of how you receive your intuitive messages
- Know how to use those intuition channels in everyday life

My Intuitive Woman Quiz

Directions: Get a pen and paper, noting your answers for each as True or False.

1. I walk into a room and immediately feel who is in a good mood and who is not.
2. I never forget someone's face, even if I don't remember his or her name.
3. When I meet certain people for the first time, I get tingles, shivers or my body temperature changes noticeably.
4. I can get an accurate impression of someone by simply hearing his or her voice.
5. I just "know" things about people before I meet them.
6. When I'm going somewhere new, I've had the experience where I just know I have to turn left even if the GPS says to go right. And I've gotten to my destination more easily.
7. Music is very important to me and I often have certain songs stuck in my head or hear them constantly on the radio.

If you answered TRUE for more than one of the statements above, congratulations! You are more in touch with your intuition than you know.

As intuitive women, there are certain ways that our intuition speaks to us. Some of us are primarily auditory, while others are very visual. Each of these ways or channels may have names with which you are unfamiliar. We encourage you to have an open mind. If there is a label that triggers you, look at the explanation provided and feel free to make up another label that works for you.

What Are Your Primary Channels of Intuition?

The root "clair" is Latin for "clear" and in the case of your intuition, it is the place where you are the most receptive or "clear" to acknowledge and notice unfiltered messages from your sixth sense, your inner knowing.

There are four primary ways that we receive our intuitive messages: Clairvoyance (clear seeing), Clairaudience (clear hearing), Clairsentience (clear feeling) and Claircognizance (clear knowing). We'll explain more below. This is about your awareness of your intuition, the label that you use isn't important.

Clairvoyance

First, there is clairvoyance or clear seeing. (If you answered true to statement #2 in our "Are you an Intuitive Woman?" quiz, you are predominantly clairvoyant.) You may receive quick images and see colors around a person. You may also be primarily visual and can remember how a person looks rather than his or her name.

For example, you're at a networking event and, for the life of you, you can't remember the name of one of the women you met. However, you can describe her to your friend as "the one with the brown hair who was wearing this amazing blue suit. I remember her business card was really unique. It was shaped like a square and had gold embossed letters on it." That is someone who is clairvoyant or who has clairvoyant tendencies.

Clairaudience

Second, there is clairaudience or clear hearing (if you answered true to statement #4 in our "Are you an Intuitive Woman?" quiz, you are predominantly clairaudient). You may hear phrases or sentences about someone or something. You may be sensitive to noises and may find environments with crowds overwhelming.

Using the same example of the networking event above, a clairaudient woman may tell her friend, "Didn't you just love his speech at the end when he said _____(you recall the exact quote or phrases that were used)? And I loved the song that they played on the break. Really got me going!"

Another example is that you usually have a song or two stuck in your head and try to remember the name of it but instead tend to remember lyrics or phrases of it.

Or, if you and a friend get into an argument, you remember exactly what she said to you and could probably share it with her verbatim or pretty close! Sometimes you may even hear a weird, high-pitched ringing in your ears and not know why, as there aren't any noises around you. You're not crazy! These are examples of clairaudience in action.

Clairsentience

Third, there is clairsentience or clear feeling. (Your dominant channel if you responded true to statements #1 and #3 of the quiz.) You constantly get "gut feelings" and tend to lead with your heart. You may be acutely attuned to how other people feel even when they don't say anything. You tend to be a people-pleaser.

This is one of the more common "clairs" or channels. An example from real life is:

You are in a great mood when you get on the phone with your best girlfriend. You've had an awesome day and you can't wait to share what happened. Then, she starts telling you about her *awful* day at work, complete with complaining about her co-workers, her boss and the traffic. You listen intently because you're such a good friend but by the time she asks, "So, that was my day. How was yours?" you are so confused, because now you feel anxious, tense and even angry. Almost like you stepped into the scene she was recounting at work and it somehow became *your* experience. It becomes difficult to remember the good day you had and even harder to feel that "good-mood high" you had at the beginning of the conversation. You feel exhausted and she feels happy and light. What happened?

Your clairsentience kicked in! You were able to directly connect with her emotions and took them on as your own, making it hard to distinguish what your true feelings are and what hers are. Also known as empaths, clairsentients have a gift for tuning into the emotions of others. By learning some simple techniques for maintaining your own energy and vibration, you can pick up on the undercurrents of a situation before it gets out of control (without absorbing them as your own) — thus, you make a wonderful advisor.

Claircognizance

Finally, there is claircognizance or clear knowing. (Your dominant channel if you responded true to statement #7 of the quiz.) You know things without knowing how you know them. Oftentimes, this information may feel illogical or random and you may blurt things out unintentionally.

For example, you are driving with a friend to a new restaurant and your GPS says, "go right up ahead," but you somehow *know* you need to go left. So, you say, "I don't know why, but go left instead. And when your friend negates you and listens to the GPS signal to turn right, there is a detour and road construction that redirects you to go back and take a left anyway.

Another example of claircognizance is hearing the phone ring and knowing exactly who is calling (without an identifying ring tone or caller ID) and say it aloud, "Cathy is calling me back." And you pick up and it's Cathy! Claircognizance is a thought that you just *knew* without knowing how you did. And most of the time, it's accurate when you follow it.

We have the ability to tap into all four "Clairs" but one or two channels tend to be dominant.

Now you're armed with some self-knowledge of how your intuition may be playing out in your life. Get ready for a big AHA!

"I Don't Know!"

When you enter the dating world, it can feel extremely overwhelming. One of the biggest gifts you have as an intuitive woman is your intuition and your Clairs. Oftentimes, we discount these gifts and say, "I don't know," when we really *do* know but we wish we didn't. So, the next time you say "I don't know," consider asking yourself this:

What DO I know to be true about this situation?

Take a moment and really tap into your four Clairs. Intuition may not always be immediate or logical. Before you ask this question, make sure that you are grounded. Take some deep breaths, get calm and close your eyes if it helps you tune out distractions. Intuition is subtle and if you create the right environment, you are more likely to hear its wisdom.

How You Can Use Your Dominant Channels to Your Advantage

Let's review the channels again.

- Clairvoyance or *clear seeing*
- Clairaudience or *clear hearing*
- Clairsentience or *clear feeling*
- Claircognizance or *clear knowing*

Once you know your dominant Clairs, you can use them to your advantage in your everyday life. Below is an example of how you could activate them in your dating life as well as your relationships with friends, co-workers or family.

Clairvoyance in Action:

On a Date: Make note of the colors that stick out from the other person. It could be something they are wearing like a blue-striped polo shirt or a color around them (in the immediate environment) that you feel defines them to you and how the date went. Our subconscious minds love color, as each color evokes a particular sensation or feeling. When you're dating lots of people in the beginning, this is especially helpful, as you'll be able to recall the date and also how you felt based on the color. Example: Dan is the guy with yellow around him. Maybe you felt really happy around Dan and this is the color that kept coming to you, so you write down "Dan-Yellow."

With Others: Let's say you and a friend are deciding between two hotels to stay at in Vegas. They are the same price, relatively same location, and you just want to make a decision. So, you check out the website and look at the colors and images of each hotel. The one that has colors that feel more alive and expansive wins!

Clairaudience in Action:

On a Date: When your date shares information about him- or herself, mentally ask: *Is he telling the truth?* If he clears his throat a lot or you get strong ringing in your ears, it could be an indication that he is hiding something or holding back the whole truth. That is your opportunity to ask clarifying questions and decide whether you want to see him again.

With Others: You can use the same line of questioning/ check in described above with all your relationships, especially new friendships or potential business partners, before inviting them into your life.

Clairsentience in Action:

On a Date: When you're out with a guy, pay attention to how your body feels after he leaves and the date ends. Is your tummy tight or upset? Do you feel light and open? If it's the latter, give him the green light for date two! Your gut feelings are in alignment with seeing him again.

With Others: You and a good friend are discussing an upcoming outing. If your body tightens in any way, ask yourself: *Is there something I want to share here?* If the tightening continues, you may need to speak what's in your heart to your friend. You may find that the tightening releases after that.

Claircognizance in Action:

On a Date: When he first comes in the door or you first lock eyes, mentally ask, "What do I already know about him?" You may get a sense that he is a serial dater, only in it for the sex, or something totally unexpected. At the end of the date, write your *knowings* down and assess whether you want to continue seeing him or cut it short.

With Others: In a business meeting, before signing a contract or even having a verbal agreement, ask yourself: *What do I already know about this situation or connection?* Write your knowings down and assess whether you want to go through with it or you need to clarify or ask a question before moving forward.

So, now let's look at an example from Diana's dating files.

The Stomach Flip: A Story From Diana

I had made a conscious effort to change my pattern of simply judging a man on how attracted I was to him physically/sexually. Sam was totally opposite of my type. He was tall and lanky with a languid way of speaking that was both unnerving and calming. I was immediately drawn to him but it wasn't the usual butterfly-in-the-tummy feeling. It was something else. My vibes told me: *You will talk to him tonight and he will ask you out. Go out with him.* Five minutes later, that's exactly what happened. He asked me out to dinner properly and told me I was the most beautiful woman at the party. It was sweet, but my first impression was, *That's nice, but I wouldn't want to kiss you.* It felt shallow but it was true. It had been so long since I was treated like a Goddess. You know, where the guy picks up the check without question, he smiles and compliments you and you feel like a queen? I knew I was a bit jaded and scarred from past experiences but I decided to give Sam a chance.

The night before our first date, I was so excited. The dress, hair and makeup were camera-ready. But I got inexplicably ill. Like stomach-flu–cold-sweat–fever ill, plus I realized that the allergy medicine I had taken was the drowsy kind. Great. I had to cut our date short but I remember one very important thing. When he went in to kiss me, I ducked and backed away. My logical mind said to him: "I'm old-fashioned. I don't kiss on the first date. Plus I feel really sick right now. Take me home."

Pause. Review time. Which of the four Clairs were being activated? No cheating!

If you said, clairsentience or clear feeling, you are correct!

Now back to the story.

Was it the whole truth? The words were true, but my body was the first and final judge. Sick or not sick, the idea of kissing him sent me into physical discomfort and pain. My intuitive woman vibes were kicking in big time! Did I listen to them? I'll save the end of this story for a later chapter. It's a doozie!

The Set-Up I Never Forgot: A Story from Diana

Now let's see a case study of a time when I *did* listen to my Clairs. When I was leading writing and theatre workshops for middle schoolers in San Francisco, one of my volunteers who came every Wednesday was Victor. Whenever I was around him, I noticed that my tummy felt relaxed. And my claircognizance told me immediately that he was someone I could trust. My mind, however, took a bit longer to catch up. I had been through yet *another* breakup (the guy actually dumped me via voicemail even though he lived seven houses down my street!) so my good friend and fellow co-teacher at the time pulled us both aside one day after a class.

She said, "Okay neither of you are saying anything so I'm just going to say it. You need to go out with each other. It's clear as day to anyone but you two so I'm going to walk this way and Victor, you take Diana and walk that way." *Can you believe it?* I was mortified and Victor just looked at his feet. But we were both smiling like idiots. And I felt this familiar feeling in my tummy like I had known him before.

Again, the phrase, "You can trust this guy," flashed into my consciousness and our first date lasted eight hours! Within the first ten minutes, I told him that I read Angel cards for people (something I was pretty tight-lipped about at the time) and he didn't flinch. He just listened, fascinated, and I found myself opening up to this man in a way that I had never felt safe to before. After that night, we were together for almost two years. And although it wasn't meant to last past that, I can honestly say I followed my gut feelings (clairsentience) and trusted what I already knew (claircognizance) the whole time. I'm so glad I did, as I consider him to be one of the great loves of my life.

Reflections

Stop saying you don't know.
What *do* you know?
It doesn't matter if what you know seems like a small, insignificant issue.

What have you *seen* that you can learn from?
What have your *heard* that you can learn from?
What have you *felt* that you can learn from?
What have you just *known* that you can learn from?

Your intuition never lies and when you learn to listen to it, you can feel it working in your body.

You *are* an intuitive woman and now you know that your dominant channels are there to help you navigate the sometimes confusing and scary world of not only dating, but life. They are always available to you if you choose to tune in and listen to them. The more you can base your dating choices on whether they expand or contract your body, the easier the game gets!

Chapter Affirmation: I am an intuitive woman.

Chapter 2
The "Ex" Energy

Maybe mistakes are what make our fate.... Without them, what would shape our lives? Maybe if we had never veered off course we wouldn't fall in love, have babies, or be who we are. After all, things change, so do cities. People come into your life and they go. But it's comforting to know that the ones you love are always in your heart.

—Carrie Bradshaw, *Sex and the City*

You're clear that you are an intuitive woman and that you need to listen to your hunches, yet you may still have moments or days when you catch yourself thinking about the Ex. At first, it may just be a passing thought or you may see something that reminds you of him. Then, there are *those* nights. The ones where you fall off the wagon and inevitably check his Facebook status only to find that he's in a relationship. Or worse, that his profile picture is not just of him but *them*. And by the way, they are married. And they have a baby. You get swept back up into the whole energy of what it was like to be with him and wonder a million things that take you out of your empowered-intuitive-woman space and right back in his energetic space. What's a woman to do?

Do you know this scene from *When Harry Met Sally*?

Sally: He just met her... She's supposed to be his transitional person, she's not supposed to be the ONE. All this time I thought he didn't want to get married. But, the truth is, he didn't want to marry me. He didn't love me.
Harry: If you could take him back now, would you?
Sally: No. But why didn't he want to marry me? What's

the matter with me?
Harry: Nothing.
Sally: I'm difficult.
Harry: You're challenging.
Sally: I'm too structured; I'm completely closed off.
Harry: But in a good way.
Sally: No, no, no, I drove him away. AND, I'm gonna be forty.
Harry: When?
Sally: Someday.
Harry: In eight years.
Sally: But it's there. It's just sitting there, like some big dead end. And it's not the same for men. Charlie Chaplin had kids when he was seventy-three.
Harry: Yeah, but he was too old to pick them up

By the end of this chapter, you will:

- Learn a simple yet powerful energy-clearing technique to send negative thoughts packing and ex energy sent into oblivion once and for all
- Learn how to connect with the spirit world (if you choose) to help you move on for good
- Learn a secret self-care bath ritual to help you clear negative energy and feel more fabulous and free

One important thing to bring up before we let go of any exes is to address why our former relationships affect us so much. Even if the relationship only lasted a few months, or you perceived it as really awful and heart-wrenching, there was a time when you really did care about him. There was some kind of payoff or you wouldn't have stayed with him. Maybe it was killer sex. Maybe you were really lonely. Maybe your self-esteem was shot and he gave you just the right compliments. Whatever your motives, it's okay! Just admit them. Admitting your motivations is where you get your power back. I learned this the hard way!

I Shouldn't Have Looked Him Up on Facebook but... : A Story from Diana

It started off innocently. I logged into Facebook on a particularly lazy night and started chatting with friends. One of them mentioned to me that they were newly engaged. After replying back with the obligatory smiley face and "congrats!", my mind wandered off to my ex, Victor. We had had a passionate affair that had ended when he decided that I wasn't The One. My heart was broken and in an act of loneliness, nostalgia and a bit of desperation, I searched for his profile. I found him. It was a newly uploaded picture and he was smiling and standing next to a jet plane looking satisfied and proud. It was just a picture. It was just a jet plane. But soon, my mind began to spin out of control.

He was successful.
He was probably making more money than I ever would.
He was traveling the world without me in a private jet and the gut punch?
He was happy, *without me.*

I began to barrage myself with questions like:
What's wrong with me?
Why wasn't *I* The One?
Who else is he taking up in those jet planes with him?
He was never passionate about what he did when we were dating. Why is he passionate now?
What's wrong with me?
What does *she* look like?
Is she as hot as me?
Does he ever think about me or miss me?
Is the sex better?
What's wrong with *me*?

This is embarrassing to admit, but that night I spent four hours on Facebook and ended up calling a girlfriend to hash out the experience and re-live it over and over.

Mind you, there was no trace of another woman, as all I had to go on was a profile picture. But if you are an intuitive woman, a picture can tell a thousand stories. The question to keep in mind is: Which story is based on your intuition and which one is based on your ego?

If the picture happens to be of an ex, it's really easy to go out of "intuition" mode and into "fear/ego" mode. In fear mode, we feel we are separate from others. We wonder about what we lack instead of what we know and what is in the present. We can focus obsessively on the past in relation to what it says we lack in ourselves now. It feels exhausting, draining and all-consuming.

Does this sound familiar?

Focusing on a relationship from the past can drain your energy now and rob you of energy that you will need to create a future partnership.

I've found that sometimes the reason breakups that happen after shorter relationships (within the first three months) are so painful is that you're leaving right at the honeymoon phase. You're leaving (or you get ditched) during the time period where physical attraction and pleasure were super high, before each of you showed your full-blown respective flaws and quirks. So of *course* it's going to hurt. Sometimes like a *bitch*. Your heart (but mostly your hormones) are pissed off that they have to get off the pleasure train! So give yourself a small break. Also, I'm sure you've heard that phrase—*some people come into your life for a reason, a season or a lifetime*—right? It's true!

Karmic Relationships: What Are They? And Were You in One?

Let's take it a step further. Sometimes we meet someone

and, regardless of how long it lasts, we feel that we've known them before. Regardless of what your stance is on reincarnation, I'm sure you've had the experience where you met someone and they just felt eerily familiar (sometimes not even in a *good* way, just a familiar way.) This could be their appearance, the way they carry themselves or if we go really deep, the way we almost automatically respond to their behaviors and choices, as if we are programmed beyond our control. Chances are, you were in a karmic connection. Simply put, these are relationships that are not meant for the long haul but are there on your path to help you work out some bigger underlying issues that will prepare you for the real deal. It's like they are these cool, but oddly shaped doors that are kind of hard to open and sometimes you have to scream to get just the right key, but you somehow *know* you have to go through them come hell or high water. Karmic relationship. Is it comfortable? Um, generally no. Is it pleasurable and painful at the same time? Almost always. What's beyond the weird doors are a colorful spectrum of many emotional highs and lows because a karmic connection pushes *all* your buttons until you become strong enough to identify and hold your boundaries. Once you are able to do that, you will learn and complete the karmic lesson and get a "pass" out of Crazy Town onto the next weird door or down the aisle, depending on where you are at in your journey. Weird doors can be really fun and once you are ready to move on, there are some specific energetic processes to help you do that.

Why We Hold On

It's important to acknowledge that when it comes to releasing an ex and moving on from any situation that has become an important part of our lives, there may be a part of you that resists the process. Logically, you want to move on, but emotionally, you may still want to cling, because there may not be something clear waiting on the other side for you. You may be afraid or nervous, and that is okay! You don't have to do it alone.

Overview of Energetic Process of Cord-Cutting: What it Means

If you are new to energetic processes, don't worry. An example of an energetic process that you may have experienced is going to a memorial service for a loved one who has passed. When we connect to someone, even if it is a relationship that has long been gone, there are ties that we still feel between us and that other person. Energetic processes deal with the underlying, buried emotions that we all have. You may have experienced feeling the presence of your ex, maybe when you've visited a place you always frequented together or smelled something of theirs, like a t-shirt they left behind. Or you have a dream about someone you were just thinking about and then the next day they connect with you. Cord-cutting is a step-by-step process to assist you with honoring your past, expressing and releasing bottled emotions (even if you don't understand them) and then moving on (if you choose to) in a safe, nonjudgmental space. Cord-cutting can help you:

- Let go of old relationship energy (or anyone who seems to have a hold on you)
- Release sexual ties to your ex that prevent you from moving on
- Call back your energy and personal power after an argument, restoring balance
- Resolve conflicts, often from a long time ago that you weren't aware of
- Raise your energy level and improve your mental clarity
- Improve sleep

Cord-cutting with the Angels is something I learned from one of my most inspiring teachers, Doreen Virtue. She describes this process in her book, *The Angel Therapy Handbook*. With this energetic technique, you are only able to release the energy that could be draining you in an unhealthy way. Oftentimes, we attach energetically because the pain of not having that person around is too difficult to bear, but it can affect your physical and emotional health.

If you're very visual, this unseen energy can resemble cords that look like long, silver ropes that go from somewhere on your body to someone else. Depending on how strong your connection is, the thickness of these cords will vary. For example, a mother and a daughter can have a very thick, dense energy cord. It's important to say up front that cords are neither good nor bad. They just represent the lines of energy you have with a particular person, object or place. Think about it though, energetic ties are why we have such strong emotions toward people even when they are nowhere near us.

There are connections of unconditional love, like the cord between you and your parents, or you and a good friend or child – even unconditional love between you and old lovers. It's important to know that we can *never* cut these cords of unconditional love. It is impossible.

Below, we will explain step-by-step how to do this if you already have someone in mind that you'd like to let go of right now, but for now you have a general understanding of the technique and can use it whenever you feel compelled. And again, if you've never done anything like this before, it's okay! You may come back to this section when you are ready. But know that with a bit of practice, consistency and faith, you can do this. You may need to cut cords on an ongoing basis depending on how strong the attachment is. This is normal. Be patient with the process.

Asking the Angels for Help: From Diana

I have found it helpful in my practice to call in the

Archangels for assistance. Now, I want to say upfront that this process of calling in Archangels will not in any way interfere or negatively impact your chosen religion or spiritual connection, whatever that may be. The intention of calling them in is to assist you with the process of moving on and beyond that, you are free to call on them for more help or not at all. The Arch-Angels have no egos. Experiment for yourself and tune into your own inner wisdom. For myself, I just know that when I call them in, I move my ego-mind aside. This helps me and my clients relax and feel safe and comforted, which is always a great place to be when you're going through any kind of transition. Again, you must follow what feels right for you always.

Michael and Raphael

The two Archangels who can help you to release old energy are Archangel Michael and Archangel Raphael. You may want to Google them if you're really interested in learning more about them, but for our purposes, Michael helps with protection, feeling safe and having courage to make necessary changes in our lives. His color is indigo blue and in pictures, he's often seen with a silver sword that is used to cut away any cords or energies that no longer serve either party. Raphael works with healers and can help with any kind of physical or emotional healing process. His color is emerald green and after cords have been cut, you may feel his soft, loving presence around your body. If you like visuals, he's often seen sealing off any areas that were released with his emerald green healing balm.

So, now that you've been introduced to the Angels and why we do cord-cutting, you can use the step-by-step process here if you would like their help with moving on from your ex.

How to Do It: Step By Step

1) Prepare your space. Create a distraction-free zone for about ten minutes.

2) Breathe deeply and close your eyes, visualizing the situation or person with whom you wish to cut cords in your mind's eye. See them right in front of you.

3) Call in the Archangel of Protection, Archangel Michael, by saying, "Michael, I welcome you to my space to help. I give you full permission to cut unhealthy cords of attachment that I have with (insert name or situation)." Don't worry about saying it "wrong." As long as you give Michael permission to cut your cords, you are fine!

4) Close your eyes and breathe deeply. This can take anywhere from thirty seconds to fifteen minutes. Some people experience tingling, temperature changes, goosebumps or just a sense of peace. Everyone is different and it's okay to feel nothing as well. The energy goes where it needs to as long as you have set your space and have a clear intent to cut the cords.

5) Speak your truth aloud: It is also normal for emotions to come up here. Let them in and know that it's perfectly okay to speak your truth or let anything off your chest about the situation or to the other person's Higher Self that helps you feel complete with them. They can hear you and they won't talk back. This really works. Example: "Dan, you really hurt me. I never understood why you didn't call me. But I am willing and choose to move on. I love myself. I let go now."

Trust that the energy is being lifted from the areas on your body that were affected by your connection and know that the space left behind will be filled with healing energy from the Archangel of Healing, Archangel Raphael. You will get a clear sense of when it is complete. Use your intuition. Some people will hear "Done." Others will literally see the energy cord lifted out of them. Still others will just "know." Trust your body.

Say aloud or silently, "Thank you Angels." And slowly open your eyes. Congratulations! You have cut your cords!

You may find that you need to cut cords more than once with one person if you have strong attachments. Listen to yourself.

After Cutting Your Cords: Recommended Self-Care from Diana

To clean your energy field, I recommend that you take a warm, healing sea salt bath. If you don't have sea salt, Epsom salt works great too. If you want to get fancy with it, you can add a few drops of your favorite essential oil and baking soda.

This bath is a ritual to honor what has passed and what awaits you. Sit in the bath for at least thirty minutes and allow your mind to wander or remember all the times you were with your ex. The happy times. Remember, this is a time of honoring the relationship, which is just as important as shedding and releasing the painful emotions. You may want to cry, laugh, yell, etc. It's okay! That's simply your body's way of processing that there has been a significant energetic shift. Release any judgments about what *should* happen.

Then, after thirty minutes, take a warm shower to cleanse

off any residual energy. I recommend avoiding technology of any kind after this, as it can disrupt your healing. My recommendation is to allow your creativity to guide you here. Maybe you want to write in your journal, draw a picture, dance in your room or sit quietly for a few minutes with a candle. It's up to you.

Consider keeping a notepad by your nightstand to capture any insights that you might have in the morning. Enjoy a full, restful sleep. If you love crystals, I recommend a clear quartz crystal along with a rose quartz pointed in the direction of your temples or third eye to continue the clearing while you sleep. Make sure the crystals have been cleansed ahead of time. You're all set!

Now, let's see what happened with our example from the beginning of this chapter with Diana and Victor.

Cord-Cutting in Action: A Story from Diana

I knew that in order to move on, I had to cut cords and release Victor from my heart. There was a bit of fear there; when you get used to having someone's energy around you or constantly thinking about them. The idea of not having him around can feel overwhelming. Think about when you lose a beloved pet. For the first few weeks without them, you may keep turning around, expecting them to be there waiting for a snack or running to greet you when you open a door. This process is about releasing grief.

I chose to do the cutting cord release described above, and two days later, I received an email from Victor after not hearing from him for more than a year.

Did I do the exercise wrong? I thought.

It was a short email.

"Hey. Just thought I'd say hello. How are things? V."

What surprised me even more was how neutral I felt. Instead of feeling pulled back into him, I felt nothing. I smiled at that, curious at my own feelings.

Which brings us to an important point. When you truly release your ex, they may sense energetically that you are moving on and may contact you to keep the connection going.

Do not misinterpret this as a sure-fire sign that you need to get back together or that you are under obligation to continue the connection. Give yourself a few days to assess your feelings. What do *you* want? How do *you* feel? It is very common for the person who initiates the release to feel nothing or to feel neutral afterwards, like Diana felt, even twenty-four hours after being caught up in ego mode or nostalgia. Energy is *that* powerful! And you don't have to stop there. Cord-cutting can be used for other areas of your life. We've listed a few below but feel free to experiment on your own and you may find that it becomes your go-to technique to help you feel more centered and happy in your life.

Other Ways You Can Use Cord-Cutting:

- You can cut cords with furniture, homes or objects that you want to sell. Even those things carry an emotional attachment.

- Cut your cords before you walk into your home from work. You will naturally clear any negative energies you may have picked up on at the office and you could feel a lot calmer and open at the end of your day.

- Cut cords with your thoughts. If you find yourself in a negative, monkey-mind merry-go-round, stop, breathe and cut your cords with that mental state. Start fresh!

Once you cut your cords and continue to check in with your body and intuition before giving in to an impulsive need to check up on your ex, your chances of attracting Mr. Right now go up exponentially. And you'll be so confident and free that you'll want to get new Facebook profile pictures of *yourself* looking fabulous! You won't have time for what's-his-name anymore or what's-her-name obsessions because you will have a new energy field that does not include them anymore. On to bigger and better, my darling. We're routing for you! Remember, your power lies in the *present*.

Chapter Affirmation: I am as intuitive as the most intuitive person I know.

Chapter 3
Cleaning House

There isn't enough wall space in New York City to hang all of my exes. Let me tell you; a lot of them were hung.

—Samantha Jones, *Sex and the City*

Now that you have looked inside and identified yourself as an intuitive woman, it's also important to look outside at your physical environment to align with what it is that you say you want. The external environment includes the things you write (your words are put out into the Universe as well as on paper), the physical space you live in (especially your bedroom and the clothes), and people (especially ones you've been in relationships with) that you invite to be a part of your experience.

By the end of this chapter, you will:

- Create a space in your home that helps you feel ready to call in love
- Learn practical strategies to clear out old relationship energy that will help you feel in control of your emotions
- Identify your core patterns and discover why you may be short circuiting yourself in relationships

Have you ever broken up with someone and had this all-out rage festival where you delete his number out of your cell phone, have a bunch of your best friends over to toast to his demise and maybe have even burned his stuff in effigy, cursing as the flames get higher like a crazy woman?

You know how that story goes, right? You feel awesome for like an hour. Maybe even for a whole twenty-four hours, or if you're really amazing, a week. But inevitably, you start feeling bad all over again. You somehow manage to go back into your Sprint account history to find his mysterious number "just in case" and you may have a good cry or worse, drunk-dial him and apologize for it, only to feel like crap right after you hear his voice. You may even reminisce about him while laying on your bed and the next thing you know, he's knocking at your door, you're knocking boots with him, he leaves and you have to do it all over again. The rage turns into sadness, loneliness, depression, self-esteem-lowering, power-sucking despair and hopelessness. The cycle begins again. Sigh.

If you're nodding *yes*, we want to give you a hug right now. We've both been through our own versions of the above. You're not alone!

It's time to claim your space and call your energy back, Goddess!

And we want to help you do that.

Are you ready?

Cleaning Up House Literally: A Story from Diana

For the longest time, I was single and I couldn't figure out why. I had done more love affirmations and mantras that I care to admit. I had been on a dating site for six months and all those dates had ended after two outings. Then, my friend and Feng Shui consultant, Andrea, asked me a key question that made me look at relationship space in a whole new way. The conversation went something like this:

A: "Diana, have you been having a lot of men who just

want to have sex with you and not have a relationship?" (My face gets hot with embarrassment.)

Me: Yes! How did you know that?

A: It doesn't take a psychic to figure that out. Look at how many nightstands you have. (She pointed to my lone white nightstand.)

D: What's wrong with it? Should I get a different color?

A: No! You're literally saying to the Universe, "Send me *one-night* stands!"

D: Oh crap, you're right! (Light bulb *Aha!* ensues. I had had one nightstand as long as I could remember. Suddenly I saw a ray of hope.)

A: So, unless you just want to get busy with these men, I suggest you get two matching nightstands and put them on either side of the bed. Maybe even get brand new ones with matching lamps. The Universe loves things in pairs for relationship seekers.

Conclusion: Andrea rocks. And time to haul my one nightstand to Goodwill.

Part 1 - How to Prepare Your Space for Love: Space Clearing with Diana

If you want to call in lasting love, an energetic process you can use to do this is called *space clearing*. Just like my nightstand example with Andrea, it is intended to help you catch things that are already in your physical environment that are out of alignment with the type of relationship you say that you want.

In this chapter, some of the tools we will be sharing with you to help you walk away from your physical space feeling confident, peaceful and ready to call in love include: Feng Shui basics, identifying your love colors, which crystals to use to call in certain types of relationships, and even the use of ancient herbs and wood to help you clear out anything that is holding you back from the love you desire.

If you are new to these energetic processes, there may be some parts of this information that are more helpful to you and others that do not resonate with you until a later time. Please don't stress about this or feel that if you don't do all of these things that your love life is going to be bad. Have you ever picked up a novel that is all the rage only to find out that you can't make it past the first couple of pages? Me too! And then, maybe months later, when things in your life have shifted, you finish it cover to cover in a single evening. Happens all the time! Your timing is perfect.

Regardless of what you choose to experiment with, a great way to begin is by first noticing how your physical environment affects how you feel. Have you ever walked into a room or in a restaurant that was full of clutter or chaos? You may have noticed that you felt on edge or scattered. That was simply your body telling you that that particular space activated a specific feeling inside of you. The techniques and tips we are about to share will help you feel balanced, more energized and clear-minded in your physical space so you can make better decisions in your love life.

Feng Shui Basics

Locate the Relationship Corner of your room (or house). You can do this Feng Shui technique for your bedroom or if you're a superstar, you can do it for your entire home.

When you come in through the door, it will be at the back right corner. This is the area where you want to clear and enhance. You should clear clutter from your entire space but especially this one! Here are some fun tips to spruce up your physical space. Include things in pairs: matching nightstands, lamps, pillows, statues of couples, two candles, pictures and paintings of two people or anything that helps you feel loved, cherished, respected, etc.—all the qualities you wish to call in for your new love.

Use Your Love Colors

Believe it or not, there are certain colors that tap into your subconscious mind to help you call in love and other colors that affect your mood, energy level and even sex drive! You can get creative here. If you aren't in a space where you can paint or put anything on the walls, getting a simple object like a pillow, candle or even lampshade will do the trick. And if you are really tight on money, you can even take a sheet of colored paper and put it in your relationship corner with the strong intention that when you put it there, you are opening up your heart. Use them in moderation. Example: If you tend to be an extremist, you may feel tempted to paint and decorate your room in one color, which can be excess and an overload to your nervous system. Use your intuition to tell you where to inject a bit of color in your space. Great colors to add into the bedroom and your relationship corner:

- Red = Passion. If you want to spice things up, add this color. But, like with everything, use it in moderation. Why? The opposite side of this color actually activates and excites (so I wouldn't recommend that you sleep on red sheets or you may have trouble falling asleep).

- Pink = Partnership and Romance. It's no accident

that you see lots of pink around Valentine's Day. It evokes timeless innocence and romantic gestures. Want to take your relationship from the holding hands stage to the hot and heavy passion? Use peach and red with your pinks.

- Peach = Ramp up your sex life! Watch out for too much peach, though, or it could bring in multiple partners or infidelity.

- Earth Tones and Skin Tones (especially for the bed itself), Browns, Greens, etc. = Warmth and Nurturing. Earth tones are fabulous for evoking the body's five senses and some Feng Shui experts say that they mimic being held in the arms of your love and connecting.

My Home Reflected How I was Losing Energy in Relationships: A Story from Andrea

When I learned where my Love/Relationship corner was in my bedroom, I gasped when I realized that it was the bathroom! I had a consultation with Diana and one of the things that came up was that while the bathroom is a place of cleansing, the constant running water and pipes symbolized emotional energy running in and out. And that is exactly how my relationships had felt. I was always giving and giving until the man left me for another woman or he would become so incredibly emotional and needy which really frustrated me! When I asked Diana what I could do to shift that around so that the energy in my relationships would be more grounded and balanced, the color red kept coming up. It is the color of passion (which I want in my relationships) but it is also a lucky color in Feng Shui that can contain any negative vibes. So, one of the suggestions she made to help me was to get some red electric tape to wrap around the pipes underneath the sink and around the toilet. I also used what I already had and put my hairspray (a red can) on the counter as well as some soothing lotions and scents that make me feel sexy that happened to have a lot of red on their containers. The result? I received an invitation from a very nice, grounded man to go listen to music and overall, the drama in my love life has left, opening up space for someone new to enter my life. Feng Shui rocks!

Color My World: A Story from Diana

I have long been sensitive to colors and I found that I was literally avoiding certain spaces in my home because of the way I felt when I stood there. Sometimes it was a clutter issue, sometimes it was a cleanliness issue, but the one constant I noticed was that my physical body would have a reaction to certain color choices I had made. I noticed this more than anything in my bedroom. At that time, I was in between relationships — not quite over the last guy but not quite ready to dive into a new thing. You know that in-between place, right? The perfect time to decorate your space! I hired another Feng Shui consultant. I love my Feng Shui! She pointed out that I had *a lot* of purple and complimented me on having matching lamps, nightstands and the position of the bed *(Thank you! Feng Shui gold stars!)*. I also had my Angel altar and candles everywhere. Right away she said, "Diana, this is the perfect room... for someone who just wants to have a relationship with themselves."

Ouch. I was so confused! "Um, well I do want to be alone right now but not forever. Can you explain this to me because I do have the matching furniture now? I've been really conscious of my space," I replied, taking it all a little too personally. She went on to say that while she understood that I loved purple, it was the predominant color in my bedroom and it represented a Higher Power/

Spiritual Life. Along with all the purple and the altar I created, I literally left *no* space for anyone else and it wasn't exactly an environment where a partner would feel comfortable to exude a lot of *um, passion* with me. *Damn.* I knew she was right.

She suggested I get some earth tones in there and I ended up with green sheets. I kept my purple comforter (because dang it, I loved it!) and moved the altar to my home office, replacing it with lovely pictures of nature scenes framed in wood. And to ramp up my passion vibe, I added a fire engine red rug on my side of the bed! The take-aways? Well, first off, soon after I was flooded with dates (which I frankly wasn't prepared for, but it's safe to say I activated my relationship space!) and I learned the lessons of moderation and intentionality with color. I also learned that I didn't need to give up my spiritual side. Instead of hiding and holding myself back from a relationship with all that altar stuff in my space, I moved it to a space where I could actually enjoy it as I wanted (my home office, which is very much my space and I commune there alone, with the doors closed). As I recall too, that week, I also booked an influx of new clients. I'm telling you, this stuff works.

Crystals to Help with Love/Relationships

If you're into crystals, check out rose quartz, a pale pink crystal that you can use by holding in your receptive hand (not the one you write with) and spend some time each day in your bedroom/relationship corner feeling the energy of the new choice you made in Part 1 and also the possibility of new love. If you would like to learn how to hold your boundaries, check out hematite, a metallic-colored stone. And finally, a good one to have in your home and nightstand is clear quartz. This helps to balance energy and purify your thoughts, which can be especially helpful if you have had a hard time believing that love would find you. Be sure to clear off the energy of the stone about every two weeks, as it can collect energy. You can do this by letting it sit in the sun for two hours or running it under warm water with intention.

Using Herbs and Wood

One of the most effective (and simple) ways to change the energy of a space is to go to your metaphysical shop and ask for an herb called *White Desert Sage* or a stick of special wood called *Palo Santo*. You'll see sage usually wound together with thread so it looks like a little wand. They have them in all sizes and they range in price from a few dollars on up. Just ask the shopkeepers and they'll know exactly what you're talking about. Warning: It smells a little funny (if you are new to using it, you may think it smells like marijuana) so if you're concerned about that, use Palo Santo because it is gentler. Palo Santo is an ancient wood from South America that is said to clear negative energy and it smells nice too! Most stores will sell them in packs of six and they're very affordable.

How to Use Sage or Palo Santo

Before you begin, open a nearby window or door so the smoke has a place to go. Also, symbolically, this action represents your intention to allow the new in and let the old stuff out of your life. Then, light the wood or the sage and walk around the space you want to clear, remembering your intent to release the old/the past as you smudge or wave it around. Make sure you take your time and hit all the corners, as a lot of stuck energy can congregate there. Once you have gone through the whole space, it's time to use the power of your words to complete the release ritual. Stand in the center of the room and share with the Universe what you want. Diana's example is below but please feel free to change the words so that they feel right for you. For example, you could say, "I now release all negative and old energy from old relationships now. I welcome in new love." The last step is to say "Thank You!" and make sure you close the door or window that you opened. You're done! You may notice an immediate shift in the way you feel when you're in your room; for other people, it takes a little bit to notice. Remember, you don't need to know *how* this stuff works. With rituals like this, all that is needed is a strong intention and commitment to opening up to the new. You did it!

Goodwill Ritual

Gather all old clothes, sheets and lingerie you wore with old relationships, and anything symbolic that represents the old. Before you go and do a rage festival (remember we learned about that before!), hold each object one by one and say the following with intent to let it go:

> Thank you for all the lessons that have come from having you in my life. I am ready to let you go and I withdraw and release all attachments and energies associated with this old connection.
> It is done.
> It is done.
> It is done.

This may bring up some emotions. Let them arise. You are more than your emotions. You may find that you want to keep some objects, as you may feel neutral. In that case, still say the release prayer and then inject a new energy. Example:

> I now command that this represents peace or security. I welcome you back as this new energy into my space now.

Take a trip to Goodwill and let it go, Goddess!

Part 2 - Taking Responsibility for Your Emotional Space

Ok, contrary to what you may think, we're actually going to encourage you to think about your exes. We're not going to say, "Forgive and forget them. Forgive yourself and it will all be awesome." Frankly, that's BS hogwash, wishful thinking and there will be none of that here.

Before you can truly forgive yourself, you have to take responsibility — full responsibility — for the choices you made in the relationships of time gone by. The common thread they have is you, so take heart because you are the solution.

A Powerful Exercise That *Will* Change Your Relationship Energy: This All Goes Back to Your Needs

Somewhere deep inside, each of those key romantic relationships fulfilled a need you had. The big needs that we all experience are:

- Feeling loved
- Feeling wanted
- Feeling appreciated
- Feeling liked
- Feeling special
- Feeling safe/secure

Here's a real life story from Rachel, whose name has been changed to protect her privacy.

Unconsciously Over-Giving: A Story from Rachel

Rachel discovered that she had a deep need to be seen as special, and in her last relationship, she *was* special. She catered to his every need, especially financially, as he was out of work. She had created a dependency, enabling him to continue to be a homebody, with no incentive to take action towards a career of his own because she was footing all the bills to compensate for this need to be special.

When she dug deeper, she uncovered that when she was a little girl, one of eight siblings, in order to receive the attention and feeling of "being special," she always had to over-give in order to stand out. Years later, it conveniently played out in each of her adult relationships until she uncovered it and acknowledged it.

Get to the Root of Your Pattern

Write down the last person you were with.

1. Ask yourself: *What need did he fulfill for me?*
   To start, you can use feeling loved, feeling wanted, feeling appreciated, feeling liked, feeling special and feeling safe/secure. Go with your first instinct without judgment. Your answer may surprise you.

2. Ask yourself: *How is that unmet need showing up in my actions right now?*
   Write down everything that comes to your mind, even if you don't quite understand it.

3. Ask yourself: *When I was a little girl, how was this need not met?*
   Emotions may arise here. Let them. It's just a release for the heart. Write down what comes up even if it doesn't make sense right now. Go deep.

4. State Your Truth Mantra: *I acknowledge that I have a need to feel _____.*
   You can do this silently or aloud. Stating your truth mantra aloud may be more powerful for you in

terms of releasing a pattern of behavior.

5. Script Your New Choice.

You've done the tough work. Now it's time to move through it. Complete and say these mantras aloud. If you want to be bold, say them into a mirror.

I acknowledge that this came from (insert your past memory) and I am aware that I made the choice to (insert how you act to compensate for that need, i.e., being a people-pleaser, enabling, over-giving, when you don't want to) as a result. I now choose a new choice and cancel this old choice. I thank it for where it brought me to but I choose a new choice NOW.

What would that new, empowered choice look like? Write it down.

Example: If you are a people-pleaser, you can choose to be an empowered woman with healthy boundaries or someone who is respected and confident. Using adjectives is a great place to start.

My name is _____ and I am a powerful woman who has healthy boundaries. I am confident and loved in all my relationships.

You may choose to record yourself saying this and play it each morning to help you get into a new place in relationships. You may even want to get creative and write a song. Whatever you choose, have fun and remember, you are calling forth a brand new pattern.

6. Take a New Action!

The last step is to brainstorm a practical action you can take in your daily life to help reinforce the need to "feel special" being met within yourself. For example, maybe having fresh flowers in your home makes you feel luxurious and special. You could commit to buying yourself flowers two times month. Write down your action now.

Little things like this add up. Maybe you think flowers are too expensive and you can't justify buying them. The return on investment that you're going to get from feeling special is well worth the few extra bucks.

Action I can take to meet my own need:

_____.

Congratulations!

As a next step, you may choose to go through all your significant romantic relationships and do this exercise. You may start to notice a pattern and you can add your relationship script each time.

Chapter Affirmation: I am able to learn from the past and use my knowledge to improve my future.

Chapter 4
Deal Breakers

Rigidity is rarely your friend, but well understood boundaries make decision making a lot easier.

—Seth Godin

What Is a Deal Breaker?

Deal breakers are the things that are non-negotiable in a relationship. Before you go on a date, it can be extremely valuable to identify what your deal breakers are. Example: If having your own children is very important to you and a man says: "I don't want to have kids," then that is a deal breaker. There is no wisdom in thinking that he is going to change his mind and it is also detrimental to your own self-worth to move forward, knowing that you will never have what you truly desire. Believe what he is saying is true, even if you don't agree with it or find it unpleasant. You wouldn't want someone to set out to change what you believe, so don't set out on a path to change someone else.

Oftentimes, intuitive women tend to be the caretakers and givers in the relationship. Stating what you want up front not only saves you time; it saves you energy and *that* is worth more than anything. When you don't listen to your own intuition, you block yourself energetically from moving ahead, not only in your romantic life, but in your career, finances and health. Everything in your life is interrelated. You'll notice that when you start using your intuition in dating more, your intuition will improve in other areas as well.

By the end of this chapter, you will discover:

- What deal breakers are and how you define them
- Why you might be compromising what you want
- How to stop putting other people's needs/priorities before your own

Defining What's Important

Defining what's important to you is the first step in understanding what your deal breakers are. Generally, deal breakers fall into major categories. The list below contains some of the major categories but is not an all-encompassing list. For instance, some men love watching sports on TV. If you hate sports, that might be a deal breaker for you. Don't feel badly if you have a long list of deal breakers. Knowing what you don't want gets you closer to what you do want. If you've just started dating after a break-up or divorce, this list will help you create terminology around your values.

General Categories of Deal Breakers

Marital Status (current and previous - relationship with current and previous mate)
Kids (having them, wanting them, age/existence of current children and relationship with current children)
Political stance
The importance of spirituality or religion
Early bird vs. night owl (differences in lifestyle)
Punctuality
Feelings about having pets
Cultural differences/language barriers
Occupation
Differences in family values
Family member acceptance (Does his mother like you?)

Educational level
Geographic location
Health
Finances/how you view money
Smoking
Drinking/not drinking
Personal hygiene
Sexual compatibility
Use of medications
Commitment to fitness
Socializing/importance of friendships

Sometimes values are confused with ego desires or superficial requirements such as physical traits. This can be as simple as writing down: If he wasn't hot, how would I feel about _____? You may have thought that sometimes you have been too superficial when someone wasn't attractive or that you just weren't giving him a chance. But you may think, *well, even if he was hot I still wouldn't like* _____. It's kind of sobering. Shallow or not, your truth may be that you really like handsome men.

A good place to start is to use your intuition to assess how important are each of the circumstances above. For example, if you would *prefer* that your date be a Republican but after tuning into your intuition, you are pretty neutral on your own political beliefs, perhaps this would not be a deal breaker. Notice your body. If your body contracts or tightens at the thought of a particular circumstance, chances are that you are identifying a deal breaker. If your body remains neutral or expands, you may have some flexibility. Remember, when we use the word "body," feel free to replace it with where you identify your intuition. Example: heart, thoughts, etc.

So, How Do You Feel About Kids? A Story from Diana

Like many women, I felt very comfortable nurturing and supporting the men that I chose to be in a relationship with, often to the detriment of my own needs, health and desires. When it came to online dating, I recall one man that I dated, Robert, who really taught me the value of listening to my intuition before I jumped in with both feet.

Robert was incredibly charming and *hot*. Ladies, do you notice how we have a tendency to change the red flag to green when a guy is extra attractive? It's like there's a get-out-of-red-flag-jail-free card. That was the situation I was in.

I somehow just skipped over the area on his profile that said he had children. After a few weird dates (one of which you will read about in the next chapter!), I was guided to look back at this and upon closer inspection, I saw that they did not live at home. I also saw a vague option like "I'll tell you later" under what he did for work. *Hmmm could he be a drug dealer?*

I had only dated a guy with kids one other time, and the kids lived in another state so I never considered that a deal breaker. Something inside of me started feeling a bit funny when I saw that his kids lived near him. It brought up more questions like, *How many children? How old are they? How often does he see them? How is his relationship with their mother? And the big one: will he make me a priority?*

I decided it was too early to ask those questions, so I rationalized away right then and there. Let's think positive Diana! He probably has one kid who is in high school who never wants to see him anyway. He probably has a great relationship with his baby mama and he will make sure that no matter what, I am number one. And he's so attractive, so I'm sure the sex will be fantastic. On to more important questions like, *What are* our *future hot kids going to look like?* I figured I'd give him the benefit of the doubt. After all, I didn't want to be too judgmental.

You would think that I would have listened to my intuition at this point, but I didn't.

As I continued to date him, I found out that he had not one, but *two* children, one of whom he saw every other weekend and the other who lived in another state and would eventually come to live with him! Another fun side effect of him being self-employed as a personal trainer and handyman was that he was constantly working. As an entrepreneur, I understand the need to hustle, but when I moved to a nearby city an hour-and-a-half away, he came to see me twice in the course of our almost six-month relationship. I see now that the writing was very clearly on the wall; I was never going to be a priority. His primary relationships were with his business/trying to make money and his children. Deal breakers! I remember crying to sleep at night because I had this weird, sinking feeling like he was cheating on me, a feeling I had never experienced in any other relationship. I started to distrust him but more importantly, I started to feel like a complete fool.

My deal breakers that I identified from that relationship with Robert include:

1. I need a man who enjoys going out to eat with me as much as staying in. I do like to be the dazzling lady about town with her man and I need a man who loves and adores me for that.

2. Whoever I am with has to have a generosity of spirit and be an excellent communicator. I am done with game playing!

3. Our relationship must take top priority. I understand that sometimes priorities shift, but I am no longer

willing to play third or fourth fiddle.

The great thing about having deal breakers is that they translate to other relationships in our lives, especially our closest friendships with our girlfriends. I mean, if you look at it, our relationships with our friends and family are just as sacred as romantic relationships and with a slight adjustment of wording for your deal breakers, you can start to notice where they are being brought to the surface for you to address. It requires stepping outside your comfort zone. As women, we are taught to create community. Back in the days of the cave women, if you didn't collaborate, you might have picked the poisonous berries while your fellow sisters knew to pick from the bushes a few steps away. The thing that a lot of us misconstrue is that if we express and act from that place of honoring our deal breakers, we will be an outcast. We will be judged. If that happens, are those people really the friends that deserve your time and energy? Let's take a look at an example from Maryellen that illustrates the deal breakers in action with girlfriends.

Consciously Uncompromising: A Story from Maryellen

This isn't a dating story but it will give you some interesting insight on boundaries and deal breakers and how they play out in non-dating situations.

Several years ago, I was in an astrology Meetup group. The leader of the Meetup was a very talented astrologer who is a former college professor and a great teacher. When the session began, we'd all get our chart and one by one, we'd all get insight into our behavior and patterns.

One of the women in the group was a triple-Aries. You don't need to embrace or understand astrology to understand this story. A triple-Aries basically means that this woman is independent and was going to have things her way! As you would imagine, one of the areas that was a challenge to her was long-term relationships. I don't remember her name so I'll call her Sheila. Sheila was in her forties, had never been married and had trouble creating long-term partnerships. I always looked at her with interest because I'm all about long-term relationships. It was fascinating to me how someone could be exactly the opposite.

Anyway, Sheila told us a story about going to the movies with her friends. They met at the movie theater and were deciding on what show to see. There were several different movies they all were interested in. Everyone was chatting about the pros and cons of the different movies and different show times. When a decision had been made about what to see, everyone got tickets and was ready to go into the theater. Sheila told them, "I'll see you when the show is over." She was going to see the movie that she wanted to see. They were all shocked and upset because they interpreted her silence in the discussion as agreement with them. Sheila had no intention of compromising what she wanted to do!

Now, we are in no way saying that you should be uncompromising in situations like this, which have negligible consequences in your life. The point is, can you imagine Sheila going against one of her deal breakers just because a guy she was dating was good looking or had a lot of money? No way! Again, it's an extreme example, but can you see how you might be compromising yourself more than you realize just because you don't want to be alone?

What Is the Difference Between a Deal Breaker and a Changeable Circumstance?

The difference between a deal breaker and changeable

circumstance can be a tricky area. You want to be open-minded, but on the other hand, not to the point where you are engaged in blind, wishful thinking. For instance, if you are a devout Christian and your prospective mate is Jewish, the chances of him converting to Christianity or valuing Christianity the way that you do is slim. How many people do you know that change religions in their lifetime? How will you feel if your mate is always excluded from an area of your life that is very important to you? Religion is probably going to be a deal breaker because it not only affects you, but probably affects your immediate family life too. If you love cats and he hates cats, that's a deal breaker. If you both love cats but he doesn't want one right now, that's a changeable circumstance.

If someone has a child from a previous marriage, his child and ex will always be a part of his life. Most likely, legally, that's the way it is. If you're willing to accept his past-life baggage, those circumstances might not be a deal breaker for you. However, the way that he deals with his ex and child might be a deal breaker. You need to be clear on where your relationship and family fits into the big picture and make sure you are both on the same page. Figuring out what is a deal breaker and what might change is not easy but it's worth taking the time to decide what are the absolute non-negotiables. Your intuition is working. If you take the time to be honest with yourself, you'll get the answer that is already there. You just need to ask the right question.

What Causes Us to Compromise What We Want?

From the time we are small children, we are taught that pleasing other people is a good thing. Initially, it begins with well-meaning adults around us teaching us how to stay out of harm's way. We learn not to put our fingers into the flames on the stove, cross the street when cars are coming and avoid playing with knives, scissors and sharp sticks. After those lessons, we graduate on to more general things that make the people around us happy. We put butter on bread instead of in our hair, eat our vegetables and stop pulling the dog's tail. Then comes the part where our family values and society norms and pressures come into play. We don't want to go to the grocery store with Mom but we are forced into going because we're too young to stay home on our own.

As we get older, we might be able to stay on our own but feel pressured to do things because the rest of the family, group or class wants to do something. Everyone wants to go bowling but you want to go to the movies. You are now making everyone else unhappy because of what you want. It's not that you hate bowling; you'd just rather see a movie. So you compromise. No big deal. Maybe next time everyone does what you want to do instead. In the grand scheme of things, bowling or a movie doesn't really make a big difference in the outcome of your life.

What about things that *do* make a difference in your life? How much do you compromise things that make a difference to you? When it comes to relationships, not all deal breakers are equal. Your mate loves Mexican food and you don't. You can order something tolerable to you for one meal. No biggie! Your mate drinks and you don't, and he always gets hammered when you go out for Mexican food. That IS a big deal! Drinking or not drinking is a fundamental life value based on a choice. We are taught from an early age that we should be agreeable and go along with what makes other people happy. However, that comes from a point in life when we do not understand boundaries. Not only do we not understand what boundaries are, we certainly don't know how to set them.

Boundaries and Deal Breakers

Boundaries and deal breakers are closely connected. You need to know what you value and stick to your guns. Is that uncomfortable at times? Yes! Do we often need to find out what we don't want to define what we do want? Yes! It's all good, but when we learn how to honor who we are, we're much more well-positioned to have successful relationships with everyone around us, not just our mates.

Do you know someone that is on a special diet? Perhaps they don't eat wheat or are diabetic. When you go out to eat with them, they order special things off the menu. They don't eat what everyone else is eating because it's popular or looks good. And if there's nothing they can eat, they don't eat anything. That's what a deal breaker is like! You've made a decision about something and you remain uncompromising about it.

Remember we've been trained since we were little, especially as women, that pleasing people around us is good. We don't necessarily have to be disagreeable with people around us, but it's okay to stick to your boundaries, even if it makes someone else unhappy or feel rejected. Reacting from unconscious patterns that we may have learned in childhood usually doesn't serve us well as adults. We need to make conscious choices about what we want and don't want.

It's also important to recognize that as you make changes in one area of your life and you start to become very successful in that area, other areas inevitably change, particularly relationships. It's like how cleaning up your environment makes you feel lighter. However you define success, consider that like many successful people, you may come to a point where you may need to break away from certain familial patterns. This is very challenging but it is a powerful choice.

It's like coming out of AA and having to say *no* to your drinking friends because you don't have a common denominator anymore. In the same vein, you may have found that your common denominator with certain friends is that you work at the same place and always complain about your jobs and co-workers. If you want to stop acting that way because you are getting out of the habit of complaining, you may need to cut ties or limit your interactions with these friends, if only after working hours. It can be very hard to do, but remember, if you want a different result, you may have to do something different. It starts with a choice of how you are being and with whom you choose to surround yourself. You may choose to end relationships abruptly, but you don't have to. You can dissolve relationships over time.

You also need to know the intensity level of your deal breaker. You can use this easy, 1, 2, 3 scale to rate your boundaries. Here's how it works:

Disappointing but not necessarily bad = 1
Not good, but workable = 2
No way in hell! = 3

Here's how the scale is applied to boundaries with mates, friends and acquaintances:

Smoking = 3 (No way in hell!)
Loves football and you don't = 2 (Not good, but workable)
Works some weekends = 1 (Disappointing but not necessarily bad)

The more 3s that you have, the more you're probably compromising your boundaries. Remember, though, you need to be brave and brutally honest and list the stuff that really counts for you. This is not about intentionally avoiding the uncomfortable questions/deal breaker traits because you want a partner so badly. Yes, it is hard to be alone sometimes. But it's harder to be with someone and feel alone, and that's what eventually happens when you compromise what you want out of fear. It's easier to cut your losses early rather than prolong a situation; that takes wisdom. If you're intuitive, you'll notice over time that the price of avoiding what you already know gets higher and higher in terms of lost energy.

Stepping Into Your Power by Acting on Your Deal Breakers: Annie

Annie was on a first date with Rick. Things started out well enough but about halfway through their conversation, Annie decided to be brave and ask some tough questions to help her assess whether or not going out with Rick again would be a good idea.

Background: Annie's deal breakers include that she cannot date a man who smokes or owns cats, because she is allergic to both of those things. The last big deal breaker she identified is that she needs to be with a partner who prioritizes health and fitness. She is a personal trainer and being fit and having someone to accompany her on her hour-long bike rides is very important to her.

When she asked Rick, "So, what do you like to do for workouts? I am a big fan of bike-riding myself. I actually really love biking with groups and it would be fun to do a race together sometime if you're up for it."

From Diana:
Personally, I would just ask: So what do you do for workouts? Then, I'd wait for a response. That would tell me everything I needed to know. I would consider it obnoxious if I went out on a first date with a guy and he tried to engage me in bike racing. Likewise, it would be obnoxious of me to suggest a Bikram's yoga challenge on

a first date.

He answers, "Does walking from my car to my office count?" He says it with a chuckle, but it makes Annie uneasy. Her stomach might get tight or she may shift her stance. Her intuition is trying to tell her that this is a red flag for her but her logical mind may try and override it because it isn't necessarily a rational response. He then changes the subject quickly and doesn't ask her anything about her passion for bike-riding.

She says nothing. She takes this information into her body, meaning she just stays quiet and pays close attention to how his response feels in her body. Is there any place in her body that feels tight? Contracted? Open? If she has a hard time taking it into the body, she could also pay attention to how his words sound. Does it sound like the truth or is there something missing? An intuitive woman knows that if something feels off, it probably is off.

Sometimes what you *don't* say is just as important as what you *do* say.

Annie notices her body contracting and the more he keeps talking, the angrier she feels. But she doesn't know why. She feels like he misunderstood or didn't care about her passion for biking enough to ask her more.

And in this case, the subtext of his answer is: I don't want to talk about that, so I'll just make a joke and change the subject. Here's the thing though: you may be thinking, *she doesn't have enough information. Maybe she should just ask him another time.*

Important Lesson: You Have Everything You Need

If there is one big takeaway from this lesson, and from this book, it's to consider that at exactly the time that you think you don't have enough information, you have *exactly* the right information! A red flag doesn't always come in the form of a big, monumental moment. Red flags are very often subtle.

Yes, she could ask another time or even more questions later in the date if she's unclear. However, the body never lies. If her body was tight, contracted or somehow compromised as she was hearing what his answer was, that's a good sign her intuition is telling her that he is not meeting a deal breaker or she's not being honest in communicating what she really wants to say. If she were to override this body awareness and power through another date or even a few more months with this guy, she would eventually start to resent him for not being into fitness at the level that she requires and then later, it would start to affect her own health and mental/emotional well being.

The truth lies in assessing how you feel in the moment and right after the date. If you get that sinking feeling like something is off, it probably is. And if you find yourself justifying someone's answers to a deal breaker that is obviously really important to you, then you're just kidding yourself and you're wasting their time and yours.

Want to know how the date ended? Annie decided that she did not want to go on another date with Rick, even though he asked her out at the end of the night. For her, the deal breaker was enough to not risk it. She knew that if she started compromising something that was really important to her now, right from the start, she would only start to resent him later. So, she opted for what we call the graceful exit.

The Graceful Exit: Words Have Energy!

Just because you know you don't want to go out with someone again doesn't mean you have to be unkind. The key is to remember that being truthful and direct garners respect, and wouldn't you want to know the truth rather than be brushed off?

In Annie's case, she was graceful and respectful in how she told Rick that she didn't think they should have a second date. How we say things, whether it's wanting to go out with them or never wanting to see them again, is important.

Sticking to Your Deal Breakers Can Score you a Hot Date! A Story from Carenda

I had recently started getting back into online dating and one of the things that I was clear about on my profile was that I would not go out with anyone who was a big pot smoker or heavy drinker. I met Jared and he was cute, funny and very eager to take me out. We went out to some cafe and had a great time. I was looking forward to the second date, and when he called me, somewhere in the conversation, he casually mentioned that he smoked pot.

My stomach got very tight and I wasn't sure what to say as I thought I had made it very clear how I felt about that.

"It's not all the time; I don't do it very much at all, but I wanted to be honest with you," he assured me.

I replied with, "Thank you so much for being honest, Jared. But how often do you smoke?" It was hard for me to stand my ground on this because in the past, I would have overlooked this and made justifications.

He got really quiet. "Just once a day. So, can I tell you where I want to take you for our second date?"

I almost laughed out loud, but I appreciated again how honest he had been. And I knew then and there that there wasn't going to be a second date. Part of me was really bummed about that because he seemed like a decent guy, but I had had too many heartbreaking experiences to override my deal breaker now.

"I'm sorry Jared, but as much as I enjoyed going out with you, I'm clear about the pot smoking and once a day is just too much for me. Good luck!"

He wasn't expecting that and even after he tried convincing me that I was being too strict, I hung up the phone feeling powerful and proud of myself for sticking to my guns.

And the best part? Literally a few hours later, I got a message from a very hot man with whom I ended up going out for awhile. He listened to all my deal breakers and said he felt the exact same way. It just goes to show you, if you refuse to settle for a date that compromises your deal breakers, the Universe will bring you an even hotter date who doesn't even blink an eye when you say them.

Carenda learned the importance of sticking to her deal breakers using clear communication and also practiced faith that something more aligned would show up.

Here are some communication tips to make you and the other person more comfortable:

Focus on how *you* feel vs. how you *assume* the other person feels. No one can argue with your feelings but they could resent you if you try to assume you know theirs.

Be clear and concise. As women, we tend to over-verbalize, especially when we feel like we might hurt someone. Just cut to the chase. Men appreciate directness. Also, if you don't have any intention of dating them, don't lead them on. You'll hate yourself for it later and so will they!

Be courteous. If you enjoyed the meal, the experience, say *thank you*.

Example from Annie:

"Rick, I enjoyed getting to know you. First dates are always interesting!" (Again genuinely thank the person. There is always *something* positive you can say.) "However, the last thing I want to do is waste either of our time." (clear) "I trust how I feel and for whatever reason, I'm just not feeling anything romantic here and I wanted to let you know." (concise)

How to Stop Putting Someone Else's Needs/Wants Before our Own:

This is a tough one, easier said than done, especially for those of you who are moms. Society teaches women to take care of everyone around them, often to their own detriment. Do you know how the airlines say: Put on your own oxygen mask before you assist others? When you deplete yourself, there's nothing left for the people around you.

When it comes to boundaries and deal breakers, not knowing them or compromising them lowers our energy. If you're wondering why you're tired all the time or why you don't have as much energy as you used to, look around you. Who is building your energy up and who is draining you? Because someone is draining doesn't mean that they're bad; it just means that they're not a good energetic match for you right now. Be bold, set boundaries, know the things that you're uncompromising about and put your needs first.

If you are afraid of hurting people's feelings, making them mad or disappointing them, you're going to end up saying *yes* when you really mean *no* and end up resentful.

Deal Breaker List: Are You Ready?

Directions: Get out a pen and paper. Take a few minutes to write down any of your deal breakers. Make sure you are grounded before you begin this exercise. Take some deep breaths, turn off your cellphone and write from your heart, your innermost desires. Don't be afraid to be specific, even if you feel that it is unrealistic. After all, until you get clear on what you will accept, you will continue to attract the same type of date that you had before. If you have made it this far, we are confident that you are ready to leave the past in the past and go towards your future!

You might need to think about what hasn't worked in previous relationships in order to be super-clear about what you do want.

Rate each deal breaker with a 1, 2 or 3 to define how important that quality is to you.

Deal Breaker Contract: Make it Official

Deal Breaker Contract

"From this day, the _____ (day)
of _____(month), _____(year),
I, _____(insert your full name)
will only allow myself to date individuals
who are in full alignment with my
high-priority deal breakers below. I will
only date individuals that are in alignment
with the energy of peace, joy and happiness.

Deal breakers:

_____
Signature

Congratulations!

To print out and sign a certificate, go to: www.
TheDatingMirror.com/certificate

Now that you've created your Deal Breaker List, copy this page and print/post it prominently where you will be reminded of it.

For an extra boost, consider writing your deal breakers on an index card and keep it in your wallet.

Important note: If you break your contract, forgive yourself but don't act surprised when a situation doesn't work out the way you think it should. Draw up a new one and start fresh. You owe it to yourself!

Dormant Deal Breakers: A Story from Maryellen

I was married for many years and never expected to get divorced. I say that because a lot of people get married with reservations and kind of half expect to get divorced eventually. The short version of the complicated story is that my ex (Steve) got seriously ill and after he recovered, he felt that he was a different person and he didn't want to be married anymore. Strangely, I had always wondered how people could leave a spouse during or after a prolonged or terminal illness. Now I understand, especially where long-term effects of medications are at play.

Health has always been a high priority to me. For most of my life, I've placed a high priority on holistic health — looking at the whole person and the cause of an illness vs. the symptom. I've certainly have had my share of health challenges as a child and an adult. I've come to view traditional Western medicine as mainly a practice of throwing prescriptions at symptoms and seeing what works. Even if a drug does work, there is usually a high price to pay with a side effect. *Side effect* is a misnomer because if you take a drug and have a reaction from it, that's a direct cause and effect.

At any rate, before divorce was looming, as we went

through my ex's health ordeal I noticed that he had a very different way of dealing with his health than I did. When we ended up at the Emergency Room (many times) I would use clinical terms that I knew the doctors would understand. Steve would correct me and make everything sound like less of a problem than it actually was. Consequently, we couldn't get the treatment we needed and would end up getting sent home with no hope for recovery.

There was a point when I was talking to a good friend of mine, Rusty. He has always been like a Dad to me. We talked a lot about what was going on with Steve and me and the difference between our philosophy about health. I was telling Rusty that I didn't believe that taking one pill after another was going to result in any kind of wellness. Then, I said something to this effect: *He can take care of his health in any way that he wants to. I think that's everyone's right. The thing is, if he wants to be with me, he can't take care of his health the way he's doing it.* To that Rusty replied: "Then that's a deal breaker."

I'm pretty sure that's the first time I heard the word "deal breaker" used in terms of a relationship. Rusty had done a lot of personal development and even though I didn't quite understand the ramifications at the time, I knew that he was right.

That was a very interesting revelation to me. Steve had never had health challenges; I wasn't able to see how he reacted to health challenges. His mindset was intolerable to me. Was it complicated by the fact that we had been married for many years? Yes, absolutely! These are the toughest deal breakers, when something wasn't a problem and now it's a *big* problem because life has changed.

We can only know what we know at any point in time. It's human nature to apply today's wisdom to the past and say: *I should have known*. The truth is that we can't know everything at once. This is the reason why it's especially important to define your deal breakers up front in a relationship and eliminate relationships that don't serve you. If there are a lot of deal breakers up front, sooner or later, there will be more, or the up-front ones will get more severe. Be bold. Act with self-awareness and break patterns of denial.

I love Steve unconditionally and always will. I'm glad he got a second chance at life. That doesn't mean that I want to be married to him or have any kind of ongoing relationship with him. Know in your heart that it's okay to love someone and it's okay not to be with them in a relationship. That is true wisdom.

Post-Date Reflection Quiz

Ask yourself these after the date. Be honest! Your first answer is correct.

1. Was there any point in the date when you heard something that made you stop and wonder what it meant? If so, what was it?

2. Go through your Clairs again. Was there anything that you felt in your body that was noticeable? Did you hear anything that made you particularly sensitive? Did you just get a general sense that something was off but you didn't know what? Did anything strike you about their appearance or your surroundings that made you take note?

3. Write it down in your journal and refer to it later.

Now, after doing this exercise awhile, it will start to become easier and easier to assess a date. But as you make shifts in your approach, you're not the only one that could be affected. Your closest friends may not understand it or you may even get the all-too common line, "You're just being too picky!" Here's how to handle that if it comes up.

What to Do if Friends Tell You You Are Being "Too Picky"

When you change any pattern in your life, you may notice that there may be certain friends and well-meaning acquaintances who tell you that you are being "too picky" or they give you advice that runs counter to your own intuition. Keep in mind that as you shift and change, you may unconsciously be bringing up "stuff" for the people in your life to deal with about themselves. Some things that may be stirred up may have absolutely nothing to do with you, so stay neutral and send them love. You can listen to their advice but be extremely mindful of your own energy. Set healthy boundaries where needed and be discerning in who you tell about this new pattern. Not everyone will be on board and you want supporters, not Debbie Downers to whom you have to explain or lift up. Get comfortable with the uncomfortable, because what you were doing before wasn't working and that's why you're reading this book.

On another note, sometimes everyone is telling you the same thing: He's not right for you. He's trouble. He's not the kind of guy that you'd want to marry. When everyone around you that cares about you is telling you the same thing, there's some wisdom in listening. You might ask yourself: What am I not seeing? The point of this story is that people change over time and sometimes, something emerges as a deal breaker that has been hidden from view.

Chapter Affirmation: I am able to release old patterns and relationships and create healthy new ones.

Chapter 5
Online Dating Intuition

Intuition is the most powerful force in my life.

—Laurie Davis, Founder of eFlirt Expert
(started her business with $50.00 and a Twitter account,
now featured in hundreds of international news media
outlets)

If you've ever been on dating sites, you've seen that they
have options to refine your searches with "must have"
and "nice to have." If you put too many "must haves"
in your searches, you might come up with no matches.
That can make you feel like you have a big L on your
forehead! Here's the thing: dating sites are using limited,
mathematically-based computer programs to pair people
with each other. Just because the dating program doesn't
accommodate all of your dating parameters, doesn't
mean that they're not important or that you're being too
picky. You don't have to lower your standards. Make
the things that are most important to you "must haves"
and be mindful of the other things that you don't want to
compromise.

By the end of this chapter, you will know:

- The #1 most powerful question that you need to
  ask when you're looking at dating profiles
- How to save yourself from heartache by learning to
  "see" profile pictures
- Understanding your deal breakers in real time

When you look at a dating profile, what *can* you know? On

one hand, it might seem like you can't tell too much about someone from their online profile. On the other hand, you can actually tell a lot about a person based on the effort that they put into their profile and the words that they choose. Instead of thinking: *I can't know much about him from this profile*, ask: *What* can *I know about him from this profile?*

The Photo

First, let's start with his photo. *Is he looking straight ahead or is he looking off to the side?* Even if he randomly selected his photo, he's telling you something with his picture. Looking straight ahead into a camera shows a certain level of confidence. *Does he have multiple pictures? Who is in the pictures with him? Where is he in the photos geographically?* Very often, people's photos will correspond with what they say. For instance, someone who writes that he likes to ski will show a photo of himself skiing. When the words people use in their profile match their photos, there's a certain congruence and honesty of that matching of words and deeds. Likewise, if all of his photos are taken with a drink in his hand, or women cut out of them, or women all around him, this tells you something too. If all his photos have sunglasses, forget about him! That's a huge red flag. He's guarded and not open. Look for congruence and in-congruence between photos and words.

This is not stuff that we made up for this book. There are areas of social science dedicated to the study of visual images and how they are perceived.

It's All About Perception

We all want to look our best and be attractive to the opposite sex. Men tend to put photos of themselves at the pinnacle of their attractiveness, such as when they had more hair or were slimmer. Many times, they will combine a younger-looking photo with some current ones. Professional photos taken for a job or website can also be a little deceiving because they might be Photoshopped. If there are multiple photos, the worst-looking photo is the way that he looks now. Otherwise, why would he add it to the mix?

Women tend to look at themselves, criticize their size and over-estimate their weight. Men on the other hand, look in the mirror and are most likely to see something much better than the actual reality. The reason for this lies in the fundamental way men and women view the world. Women tend to look at the whole picture and focus in on the negative. Sorry ladies, but this is true! We like 75 percent of what we see in the mirror but focus on the 25 percent that we feel is flawed. Men, on the other hand, tend to compartmentalize what they see. They will focus on the parts they like and praise themselves for that; this phenomenon actually works in our favor. When they look at us, they focus on what they like and ignore the rest. That means they are thinking about your great breasts, not your cellulite. On the same token, he's probably looking at his best feature, overlooking his potbelly or receding hairline.

With this in mind, consider that there might be some blatantly deceptive intentions with photos on dating sites. However, another part of what might be going on is focusing on the positive. Online dating is a game of perspectives.

Like Attracts Like

The same way that you don't appreciate when someone misrepresents themselves, men don't appreciate it when you misrepresent yourself. That means you shouldn't post a photo of yourself when you were younger or thinner. Like attracts like. You don't attract what you want; you attract what you are. If you are being deceptive, that's what you'll get back. Everyone is a mirror. Energetically, this can play out in different ways. For instance, let's say that you're filing for bankruptcy and you're hiding that fact. You may attract someone that is deceptive about his age or weight. This is not to say that you have to broadcast the less appealing aspects of your life. Just be honest with yourself about where you are. Until you do some work on yourself and raise your vibration, you're not going to attract a millionaire.

What Else Can You Tell from an Online Profile?

How much of the profile did they fill out? Is it just a few sentences? Do they talk about themselves and what they want or talk more about the kind of woman that they want? What is his username? Badboy69 tells you who he is; it's not just a cute moniker. Take that kind of stuff seriously as a sign. *Is the photo close up or far away?* There is a social science called semiotics. Semiotics is the study of the way signs, symbols and visual images are perceived. Graphic artists study this field, which is why they are better at graphics than the rest of us. Anyway, on an unconscious level, pictures are telling us things, and this is not limited to formal advertisements. Be open to *seeing* what is right in front of you.

Intuitive First Impressions

What is your first impression of the profile, besides the way he looks? Later in this chapter you'll read an example about a first impression that was spot on. Your first impression might seem random, but we assure you, it's not. On a subconscious level, you know and recognize things. Pay attention to those signs!

Just remember, this book is about helping you become empowered to tap into your intuition and inner wisdom so that you don't get drained energetically and spend months or even years pursuing relationships that don't serve you. Sure, we know you get tired of waiting for The One and you get lonely on Saturday nights when your friends are out on dates. Build your support network with great friends with whom you can do things. You'll want to keep that network intact even when you are in a relationship. All of your relationships have an energetic cost. You want to make sure that the choices you make are building you up and not breaking you down. This is about approaching dating with your eyes open. Your first impressions count, even if they're online.

Is Your Intuition Saying to Jump In or Hold Off? A Story from Diana

Remember Robert from the last chapter? There's more to that story!

To refresh your memory, he was the guy with kids who I met on a dating site. Anyhow, remember how I shared with you that when I first saw his profile, I glazed over the fact that he had kids? Well I also remember thinking it was weird that his main profile picture had him looking off to the side with a sideways smile that felt like a smirk. You learned all about the profile earlier; I ignored my feelings that something wasn't quite right.

After our first date, he asked me to come home with him after our coffee and my first major red flag waved itself. My entire tummy got tight but I fluffed it off and thought it would be charming to play hard to get. So I said something like, "I'd *love* to see where you live... another time." I should have given myself a serious gold medal for self-control and called it a day, but I kept talking to him. Fast-forward to dates three and four. It was really bothering me that he hadn't taken me out for a proper dinner, where he paid and I felt incredibly beautiful, sexy, desired, all the good stuff. He had skirted around the issue of having to actually take me out. He had no problem cooking up a gourmet meal of lobster and the whole nine yards at his home, but whenever I brought up the fact that I enjoy being taken out to a restaurant, he would change the subject. I would feel guilty and weird for wanting what I wanted: to be shown off on the town with a man who was happy to be in my company. I stayed quiet and told myself that I was being silly and too needy. It was only when Robert got the hint that I was not going to sleep with him until I was good and ready that he surprised me and said he had made a reservation at a nice Italian restaurant for us and that I should dress up. I should have seen the writing on the wall but I was super excited that he could finally be getting the hint, but there were a few elements of that night that were more red flags for me.

First, he insisted that we take *my* car, which was really weird since I was always driving at least twenty to thirty minutes to his place. Red flag #2! Then, when I drove us there, I realized that the restaurant was walking distance from his home, weird again! And it was a family Italian place with kids running around everywhere so I could barely hear what he was saying. Then the kicker was when we got back to the car. I had gotten a parking ticket for parking it the wrong way. I didn't see the sign, so this was my fault but I felt really annoyed. And the next morning, I got *another* parking ticket outside his home because he never gave me a guest pass to put inside. Red Flag #3!

This was a karmic relationship, which I define as a connection where you seem to almost be addicted to each other, even though you know it's not good for you. There is an inexplicable attraction that is not always sexual but a lot of times is. It can also be extremely draining. Until you learn the lessons you are each meant to learn, you go back for more.

To make a long story even longer, after doing the karmic breakup-get-back-together dance several times, we made amends and went our separate ways. I am grateful for that relationship as it helped me clearly define my deal breakers so that I could be aware of them the next time around.

Your First Impression Is Right, Even if You Don't Understand What it Means: A Story from Maryellen

Shortly after I was separated from my long marriage, I innocently forged into the online dating world. The whole experience was pretty exotic and fun to me, something I had only heard about and had no clue how to navigate. The last time I had dated was when I was in college.

One man's profile photo caught my eye and I thought: *He's pretty cute.* My immediate impression even before I read his profile was: *He's kind of arrogant.* There was nothing in particular that made me think that. It was just an impression that I had. I fluffed it off. What the heck, I thought. I'll send him a message. He lived about seventy miles from me but as it happened, I had a nephew in the same town in which he lived and went up there from time to time. The message I sent was fairly simple and said: *Perhaps we can meet for coffee sometime.*

It was right before Thanksgiving and the thought of not being alone at Christmas was exciting. Peter thought I was pretty cute too. We instant-messaged each other online for several days and emailed back and forth. I'm not sure if we talked on the phone at all but after a week or so we were dying to meet in person. He drove down to my town on a Sunday and met a friend and me at Barnes and Noble. When we took our first look at each other there was that magic that we all hope for, the magic of: *This is the one, I'm in love!* I was on Cloud Nine and could not stop smiling. A whirlwind romance ensued and he started talking about me moving in with him within a couple of weeks. I was still in graduate school, had to sell the house my husband and I lived in and was remodeling another house that I was going to move into. In retrospect, I realized that my situation was very transitory and I fit very easily into Peter's life. He assumed that I'd move to his town when I got out of graduate school.

Peter had two teenagers for whom he had joint custody and saw every other week. He wanted me to meet the kids right away. Not having had any experience with dating, this didn't seem to be a red flag to me, but in retrospect it was. I just figured that his kids were important to him and he wanted whomever he was dating to get along with his kids. That was understandable. In addition, Peter told me that his kids hated his ex-girlfriend and that was a problem. They wanted assurance that I was not like her.

I met the kids and loved both of them! Right after that I was introduced to his entire family the week after Christmas. It was awesome to be in a family again, especially after I had just lost my relationships with my ex's clan. Everyone seemed very enamored with me and it felt great to have such approval, especially after being rejected dramatically and abruptly by my ex.

There were so many red flags waving it is hard to remember them all. I was very naive and inexperienced in dating and took everything on face value. Peter talked bitterly about how screwed up his ex-wife was. I had met her a few times but neither of us said anything much. That relationship was a new level of awkward for me. I did think several times: *She has such great kids, so she can't be all that bad.* He spoke ill of his ex-girlfriends. He mocked people that were obese, which really bothered me. He happened to be naturally thin as was his whole family. I just didn't know what to think. I was so in love, I'm not sure with what, I didn't see who he truly was.

When we first started dating he would talk about not wanting to *scare me off.* I realized later that he had been divorced for five years and had a whole lot more time to process his situation than me, unexpectedly separated for just a few months.

There was a point when my life got very tough managing the sale of the house and remodeling the house I was moving into. Instead of being a comfort to me, lending a sympathetic ear, Peter withdrew. He wasn't as available as he had been at the beginning, he didn't text as much or return my phone calls sometimes, and it was very upsetting and disconcerting to me. All of a sudden, I started hearing from him all the things that were wrong with me or the way that I was living my life or what I *should* be doing. I was so confused and hurt.

Finally, after about seven months, I ended the relationship because I didn't like being ignored and criticized. It felt a lot like how my ex-husband behaved and it didn't feel good. I was confused, devastated and profoundly lonely. How could something that started out so passionately be so different in such a short period of time? In the coming months and years, I learned a lot about myself through that relationship.

Peter was a lot like my ex-husband, except he was in such a different package, I didn't recognize it. Don't you hate that? Same person, different package — it's a definite dating hazard. They were both critical of me when anything I was doing cut into their goals or lifestyle. I happened to read a magazine article in *Psychology Today* that said that our brains will get imprinted with a certain behavior and subconsciously, we'll pick the same kind of partner because that's what we're familiar with. Oy! That was truly distressing to realize. I was reacting subconsciously.

There was one area in which I did react consciously with Peter. I never introduced him to my older brother who has high-functioning autism. I had plenty of opportunities to introduce him, but I didn't. After we broke up, I realized that I feared that Peter would not be compassionate towards him, not only because of his autism, but because he's overweight. I came to realize that an immediate gauge of someone that I was dating was: *Could I introduce this man to my brother?* If my answer to that question was "no," there was no hope for a relationship. What questions do you have like that? If you're saying something like: *I could* never *introduce this guy to my Mom*, you're saying something loud and clear that you're not listening to.

Looking back at Peter's profile, I remember reading the first line again and it seemed totally different than when I initially read it. It said: *My family comes first.* The implied message there is: *You're always going to be second.* And I was! Even on my graduate school graduation day, which happened to be the same day as my friend's wedding, I had to go to Peter's house to spend the night because he didn't want to ask his ex-wife to take the kids and because of his son's skateboarding activities. All I wanted was one special weekend with Peter to celebrate and that was too much to ask.

One of my deal-breakers became not dating anyone with kids younger than high school living at home. I realized that I wasn't willing to compromise my lifestyle for decisions someone made many years ago with another person that had nothing to do with me. In addition, I didn't want the heartache of getting attached to younger kids and then not being able to see them anymore. Peter initially wanted me around the kids and for us to be a family as much as possible. When things went awry, he acted like he had to protect them from me; the same way that he acted with his ex-wife.

If someone talks bad about their ex, it speaks volumes about them. They see themselves as a victim rather than someone who is responsible for their behavior. Going back even further, I think about my first impression. Without meeting him, talking to him, texting or chatting with him I thought: *This guy is arrogant.* I was right! Your first impression is your first impression, and it doesn't have to be in person. Trust what you feel energetically.

I didn't understand *how* arrogant he was and blindly looked past his character flaws. I attributed all my good qualities to Peter. And if he didn't have those qualities, I *assumed* that he aspired to them. That's not the way it works, ladies. We are who we are and the people we meet are who they are. Men especially will tell us who they are when we meet them. *Are you paying attention?*

Do not take on an emotional project!

Gratitude and Heartbreak

I'm grateful that I met Peter when I did, even though the relationship didn't last long term. Learning more about myself and what I want will make me a better mate when I do find a great guy. It took me a long time to forgive Peter and myself but the truth is, we were both doing the best we could at the time.

No one wants to set themselves up for heartbreak. I was too naïve at the time to know what was happening, but I'm more aware now. This is not to say that I won't get hurt, but I won't get hurt as badly and have learned to cut off relationships way sooner than I would have in the past.

All it takes now is a few hours (or minutes) and I know where I'm at with someone. It's a case of using courage and confidence rather than succumbing to fear and doubt. In the long run, courage and confidence will always serve your highest good even if the price is some short-term loneliness.

Rear-Ended by the Universe

Interestingly, about two weeks after I met Peter, I got into a car accident. I got rear-ended by a dump truck. My car was totaled but luckily, I was okay. However, I remember being overwhelmed with emotion that if something bad had happened to me, I wouldn't have had the chance to get to know Peter. In retrospect, I see the fact that I got rear-ended as a big sign from the Universe that there was something that I wasn't seeing. The fact that my first thoughts were about Peter was also a sign to pay attention to my relationship to him. I just didn't get the meaning.

"Offline" Red Flags Waving and Lessons Learned: A Story from Natalie

I met my ex-fiancé Larry at work. He was significantly older than me. How much older I did not know until our first date, after I asked him out. There were twenty-four years between us and he had three kids. Despite this latter piece of information, I still pursued him. There was so much about him that I was enamored by: his love of learning, his deep spirituality, his health consciousness, his big dreams of the future and his passion for love. Everyone was shocked that I was dating someone that much older. Even I was shocked, as I had never been attracted to older guys. On the contrary, I usually liked them young. However, I see now how "love blinds" as I was so desperate to be in a relationship that I jumped at the first person who truly showed their interest in me regardless of the warning signs.

At twenty-six, I had never been in a long-term relationship and Larry was the first guy to worship the ground I walked on. Despite the various red flags, I forged forward. And by red flags I mean not being able to go away on weekends because of his kids, realizing the story he told me about being separated was not entirely true, and constantly having to defend against his strong opinions about my choice of extracurricular activities. There were good times, don't get me wrong, and he did sacrifice a lot for me. Unfortunately, those sacrifices still did not soothe my doubts and insecurities, and given that this was my first real partnership, let's say I had a ton. My relationship with Larry was like the tumultuous ones you read about in romance novels. We were together for two-and-a-half years and I knew six months in that I should not be with him. However, I was blinded by his love for me.

Eventually the red flags became red flares: he was uncomfortable with me going away on trips; he was unhappy with time I spent with my friends; he did not understand how hard it was for me suddenly becoming a step-mom. So many times I knew in my gut that I should leave, or not buy that house together, or not loan him the money, yet I did it anyway.

If I have a regret, it is that I did not listen sooner to my intuition and consequently dragged our time together way longer than I should have.

If He *Seems* Creepy, He *Is* Creepy: A Story from Maryellen

When I first started online dating, a man sent me an instant message to start a conversation. When I looked at his profile, my immediate impression was that he was very handsome. However, in the very same split second, for no apparent reason, I thought: *That's not him.* At the time, it was a strange thought. The photo was taken from a little distance and his head was turned to the side.

Fairly soon after we started chatting, he asked me to move from the dating site to online chat where we continued the conversation. Not long after that, he came on very strong with compliments. He seemed to be fairly successful and said he was a widower with a daughter. His wife had died in a car accident. I wasn't particularly impressed by anything that he said but he seemed intent on engaging me in conversations. In retrospect, I understand that the way he portrayed himself was in a way to evoke emotion. That's a form or manipulation that can cause you to dismiss your intuition.

At one point, he got over-the-top excited about us being a couple. It was way premature. We hadn't even talked on the phone. There were little things that were bothersome to me. For instance, his grammar was a little off. I might be a little overly sensitive because I'm a writer but it still bothered me. I don't remember if he told me something about his education or language that might justify his misspellings.

At any rate, there was a point when I thought to myself: *This is either a scam or someone who's really needy.* I didn't want anything to do with either situation. I stopped corresponding with him and didn't think much of the situation.

Down the line somewhere, I remember reading a dating profile that was very similar to the guy who seemed creepy. At that point, I remember thinking that it was some kind of scam. Looking back, I realize that without even realizing it, my intuition was working when I thought: *That's not him.*

Almost five years later, I was on Skype with a friend catching up after having lost touch for a while. I was filling her in on the details of my romantic life and then asked her about her romantic life. She became visibly uncomfortable and I knew she was going to tell me a story of heartache. I listened with compassion.

My friend went on to tell me an extremely elaborate online dating story about someone she had a romance with. The details of his work and his profile were extremely similar to the details of the creepy guy's profile. The thing is that my friend got much further into the relationship than me. She had spoken to the guy on the phone many times before they were supposed to meet in person. When the day came for him to show up at the airport, he didn't show and there was no call or email. Within a few hours, after enough time had elapsed to be worried sick, a call came from some supposed kidnappers in a foreign country demanding a ransom with a threat not to go to the police.

While this might not seem very convincing the way I'm writing it, there was an extremely elaborate story that went along with the situation and more than one person involved to make the scenario believable. For instance, the man had an adult daughter in London who did chat with my friend on Facebook periodically. My friend also checked out the name of the company and locations of businesses the man worked at and everything checked out.

Luckily, my friend did not part with any money and went to the police. I don't know if anything ever got resolved. However, if you research online dating scams, you'll find sites that describe all sorts of scenarios where innocent, vulnerable people fall prey to professional con artists. It broke my heart to hear her describe what happened as *psychological rape*.
My guess is that if I went to her and asked her the first

impression that she had about the situation, it would be something related to distrust or unbelievability. Please understand that I am in no way putting her down or judging her. I know what it's like to be lonely and feel the exhilaration of relief from that loneliness. We've all had our hearts broken and it is hard to tell when we're being cynical or guarded. We all want to think of ourselves as being open to romance. The thing is, when you are lonely, that's one of the times when you're most likely to make excuses for someone, not listen to your intuition or compromise deal breakers.

My experience in life has been that the more I ignore my intuition, the more painful the lessons I get are. Now, if I get an intuitive hit that I shouldn't be around someone or do something, I act on it. I might not understand why I'm acting on it at the moment, or ever understand for that matter. But the potential price of the lesson I might learn ignoring my intuition seems too high to take a risk.

Yes to Online Dating Success: A Story from Maria

I was married for many years and after getting divorced, I realized I had no idea how to date! I had simply been out of the game too long. So, I contacted Diana who was raving about online dating and she helped me set up a profile. I thought: *What the heck? I have nothing to lose at this point.*

Well, I decided to use a pseudonym for my username, Yesmin. I had always loved that name and even though my sisters thought it was funny, I went with what felt good to me. I wrote my profile from my heart and was very specific about what was unacceptable to me. I wanted a man who was spiritual but not religious and this perhaps was my biggest deal breaker.

What happened? Well, I got a lot of interest, which was

exciting, but none of them were quite what I was looking for. There was the Bible thumper who wanted to know more about my relationship with the Holy Spirit and that was too much. Then there was the guy with a picture of himself holding a rifle. I said I wanted a man who was kind to animals and had a peaceful heart, so he was out too. And after letting it go for a few weeks, I got a message from a man who was everything I was looking for and more. Sexy, strong physical build, a professor, ambitious but kindhearted, divorced and emotionally available. And he said he talked to the stars every night before going to bed because it helped him feel connected to the Universe. I had met my match.

My favorite part of the story?

After we had gone out a few times, he shared, "Maria, do you know why I messaged you right away, other than the fact that of course you are beautiful?" No, I said. Why? He smiled and his eyes twinkled. "Because when I saw your username, all I saw was the word *yes* over and over again. And I knew I had found you. *Yes*-min.

It just goes to show you that there really *are* great men out there, even if you have forgotten to believe in true love.

Alone for the Right Reasons vs. With Someone for the Wrong Ones: A Story from Phillip

I entered the world of online dating when I separated from my wife. I was happy to discover the online dating world because I liked the idea of creating a profile and having the time to think through what I wanted to say about myself. Equally, it was nice to read through profiles and see what women revealed about themselves. In the early days of online dating, the structure was pretty open, mostly just photos and an essay. Now the online services are much more sophisticated and refined. Since my separation and divorce, I have met women both online and offline, with much greater success using the online process, especially as I got more honest about who I was and what I really wanted. One of the relationships lasted nine years and produced my daughter. Her mother and I are still very good friends and successfully co-parent, even better than when we were together romantically. My current relationship is also with someone I met online and is amazing. I attribute my success to the ideas written about in this book, though I was learning and using them before this book was written, which is why I know they are the right ideas.

There are many different ways to enter the online dating world. First and foremost, you have to be clear about who you are and what you want. It's not nearly as easy to do as it is to write that previous sentence. Once you get clear, you need to determine the right dating site to get your best results. Dating sites range from purposefully cheating, to happily-ever-after marriage, to mainstream just looking for a date. I found highly intelligent people on one site and enjoyed the question matching system.

Now, let me get back to my "you have to be clear" statement. When I first started writing my profile I was intuitively aware of certain deal makers if I wanted to have a shot at the largest group of women. These included things like "love to travel, have a good job, wants kids/ more kids, looking for The One, similar religious beliefs, similar political beliefs, and loves dogs." If any of these are not a solid fit, you can rationalize them away with the following statement, "with the right woman, I might want… kids, or to travel all over the world, or accept her Catholicism (and she would accept my agnosticism)." You see, when I am really honest, I have to put in my profile that I do not like to travel, preferring to stay close to home and enjoy local events and activities. I am a cat person.

I have a child, but do not want anymore. I was married once and have no intentions of re-marrying. I am spiritual, but not religious (love that category phrasing because it suits me perfectly). For fun, I looked into a dating site that touted over 3,000,000 members. Before joining, you could set up a basic profile and actually see where you ranked. I did my super-honest profile and earned a ranking of 2,658,802. On other sites, I've had to extend my range to 500 miles to get ten profile hits. It's not easy being me.

After a ten-year marriage that went on for seven more years than it should have and a great nine-year relationship that transformed as needed at the right time and in the right way, I have come to the skill and honesty to interpret relationships for what they are and can be. I can now read online profiles and spot the red flags quickly and have the strength to move on even if I find the person in the photos extremely attractive or other parts of the profile very inviting. It's not an easy integrity to hold, especially when feeling lonely, but I've learned that some short-term gains can result in some very long term pain. For the profiles that did not raise red flags I sent messages and hoped for contact. No matter how you slice it, and generally speaking, men pursue and women weed out.

When my daughter's mother and I separated romantically, we each set up new online profiles. I basically had to scratch and claw for any kind of response, and I know how to write a good hello note. She was on for two days and had over 200 responses (that is not a typo). Granted, about 180 of them were, "hey!" and "you're sexy!" ignoring everything she wrote in her profile and simply responding to her picture.

If you are an attractive woman within any range of the standard, be prepared to get bombarded with emails from your post. I actually started looking for profiles without pictures where the woman said, "write something intelligent, and if I like it, I will respond and with my picture." When I met my daughter's mother, I was actually only searching profiles without pictures, but with descriptions of the body type I like (athletic). As it so happened, she actually tried to post a picture, but the images were too dark and rejected. Once she sent me her picture and told me she meant to post it, I warned her that she could expect an avalanche of email (she had the girl-next-door look locked down). She posted her pictures and that's what she got, an avalanche!

Between my marriage and my second long-term relationship, I was more honest, but still fudging. After several months of dating, both online and off, I met a woman in Greensboro who bartended where I used to eat dinner before going to teach my graduate school class in the English Department at UNCG. We had a very strange first lunch date that was a classic mix of "holy crap, I'm attracted to you" and "Danger, Will Robinson, Danger!" Our physical attraction proved far stronger than my principles and I fell headlong into a passionate love that burned away all other resistances. We talked marriage and kids and I tuned out our religious differences, our political differences, and our life path differences. Yes, the sex was that good. Fortunately the Universe bailed me out and things ended between us about two months after they started. I decided to take a hiatus from dating altogether and basically get my act together.

For four months I worked on me, first by mourning the ending of my marriage. Even though it was something I had wanted for a long time, a lot of years of my life were bound up in that particular journey. Then I did some deep cleaning, emotionally and physically. I cleared out relics of my past relationships that really offered me little more than painful memories and represented energy in my life that took away from the energy I wanted to share with someone new. When I say deep cleaning, I mean I threw out all my wedding photos and love letters. I kept the poetry I wrote, but everything else went to the trash bin or in a yard sale or to Goodwill. I spent time writing and rewriting my online profile until I felt I had something that was the best reflection of who I was at that time. And lastly, I got good with one principle idea.

I would rather be alone for the right reasons that with someone for the wrong ones.

I needed to be happy with me and invite someone to join me on my journey — and that person needed to be happy with herself. Once I reached that place in my heart, I was ready to go back into the dating world and I started over.

Looking at personals with a clear vision of myself led me to avoid all kinds of profile red flags. Some were flags everyone should avoid, the main profile picture with someone cut out or the crappy snapshot. If you don't take the time to put a good photo up, you are sending me a clear *avoid* signal. During this segment of my online dating process I started seeking profiles without pictures, using fairly sound logic that a woman who knows she is attractive and wants more than a three word email is probably better off holding back her photo. Now, on the flip side, sorry guys, but we must have a photo, and a recent one; otherwise, you will hear the crickets chirping in your inbox. As it turned out, with this approach and my new focus, my first hit was the woman I ended up having my daughter with. We had a great romantic run for nine years and still have a great friendship. In that nine years many things about myself had changed. When it came to jump back into the dating pool, I had a lot of new material to work with, but the same principles applied. Be honest, no settling.

As I started dating once again, I found an odd occurrence pop up. I would meet the women whose profiles gave me hope or go out with someone I met in person and I could see the ending at the beginning. Intuitively I knew how long each relationship might last and whether or not it would be good for both of us knowing it had a shelf life. In most cases it was a one-and-done date or we actually sidled over to a friendship, a couple of which are still going strong. I did meet one woman and we fell conveniently into a "friends with benefits" scenario until she could work out her feelings for her old boyfriend. They got back together and I was happy for them both. No more benefits; and, unfortunately, no more friendship. But we both helped each other with some healing. Soon after, I was back in being-happy-alone mode, which seems to be the time when a really good relationship presents. And one did.

A possible match came up on one of my accounts. The photos showed a woman who could get dressed up and play in the mud. Really, there was a photo of her out on the town in a very nice dress and her running a race in a mud course. It was the mud race shot that really caught my eye.

This new woman was a recent transplant from New York and was looking to date only men who had children. Not only did I qualify on that front, but I was and still am the primary caretaker of my daughter, having earned my thousand-diaper-change Eagle Scout badge! Not only was this woman an athlete, but she was actually a former physical education teacher. After my not very athletic ex-wife, I made sure that one of my profile must-haves was someone I could do some kind of sport with—running, golf, tennis, biking, weightlifting, and so on. Here was a woman I could do most all of those with! I emailed her and she emailed me back; we quickly moved onto a phone conversation, then decided to meet up a couple of days later. Neither of us, as it turned out, was the type to drag things out. The one thing you cannot get online or over the phone is the physical chemistry; that has to happen in person.

One of my most painful online dating lessons came when I made a connection with a woman after my separation and before the firestorm woman in Greensboro. On the computer and through email we were a great match; physically she was very attractive to me and must have liked my photos enough to want to make the date. However, when she showed up and I opened the door you could feel the chemical thud in the air around us. We both had accurate profile pictures, but there was no sizzle between us. None, dead air. We should have shook hands and said goodnight. Instead we went out for dinner and did our best to slog through a conversation. It was misery from both sides. Until a person is in front of you, you really, really don't know. Like it or not, we have to smell each other and feel how our energy fields interact. There's no substitute for human contact.

That lesson is forever embedded in my dating psyche. So now, I keep meetings less "datey" and I suggest coffee or dessert. In the case of this new woman, I suggested frozen yogurt at an open mall near each of us. When the day arrived to meet, she had been out for a run and I was between clients, so our window of opportunity was limited. She texted me before our time to meet to let me know she needed a shower, which would cut well into our time, or she could just come on and I could see her in her after-run, sweaty glory. I figure if there's a chance we may be running or biking together, I might as well get the full on right at the start, so I encouraged her to keep our arranged time and meet me without the shower. Honestly, I was impressed I was given the choice as much as I was by the fact that she agreed to meet right after her workout. I had had a primping wife and didn't care much for it, so meeting someone willing to give me the raw version was, well, exciting.

We met, and as much as the thud was there for the one woman, a zing was definitely there for this woman. Her energy pulsed in a way that mine understood and found immediately attractive. Pleasantly she was close to my own age, so we had plenty to share about music, movies, and growing up in general. There was ease and flow; more importantly we had children near the same age and could talk about our parenting experiences and philosophies, which proved to be very similar. We have been seeing each other for over two months and, so far, it has been truly wonderful — fragile due to circumstances, but powerful and solid in terms of our feelings for each other. After our first few conversations and our in-person meeting and more conversation, I could not see the ending. Instead, I could feel open vistas, possibility, and a long future. That's how I knew this relationship was the right one for me to cast my whole heart into, and that's what I am doing.

Reflections

Be willing to ask yourself: What do I know right now about this person from his online profile? Be willing to answer honestly about your first impression.

Take note of the physical symptoms that you have when you're with someone. If you constantly have a stomachache, headache or are yawning around someone, that's not a coincidence. It doesn't mean the person is bad, but it does mean you need to pay attention to what's happening energetically.

If you want to attract a different kind of relationship than you've had, you need to work on yourself authentically to become a bigger, better version of yourself. Yes, we *know* it can get lonely while you're doing that! Loneliness is a state of emotion, not a state of circumstance.

The way someone talks about their ex speaks volumes about *them*!

Using Your Clairs in the World of Online Dating

Below are some tips to help you use your Clairs to navigate the world of online dating. Remember to have fun!

When you browse a dating site, if you are primarily clairvoyant, you will get an instant "hit" when you SEE their profile picture. Record what you notice when you look into their eyes.

If you are primarily clairaudient, then you can look at his profile, read it aloud and then notice what messages come through immediately after you HEAR yourself reading it.

If you are primarily claircognizant, scan the entire profile and ask aloud, "What do I already KNOW is true about this person?" Record what you notice and then cross-reference.

If you are primarily clairsentient, read through the entire profile and look at the pictures, paying attention to your body and how it FEELS. If it expands, notice where. If it tightens, notice where too.

It's gut check time!

After you go through this, do the basic-intuitive-gut check: Look at your responses and ask, "Is this a good energetic match for me?"

"Do I feel more excited and energized?" or, "Do I feel compromised and tired or confused?" If you get a *yes* to the latter, move on now and be okay with it! We don't care how hot he is or how many planets are aligned with yours. He failed the gut check, which means he is *not* in your dating pool.

If he *is*, congratulations! He has made the first cut.

Chapter Affirmation: I respect and listen to my intuition, even if it doesn't make immediate sense to me.

Chapter 6
Listening to Your Intuition

What does your gut tell you?

—Carrie Bradshaw, *Sex and the City*

Everything is energy and energy is everything. Think about that. Without energy, your life lacks quality. That's why when you're sick it feels so bad. You don't have the energy to do the things that you want to do in life. Mental energy affects physical energy and the reverse is also true.

When it comes to energy, there's no greater area that affects your energy than the relationships you're in. When we say relationships, we mean relationships with men *and* women. We've all had the experience of being in a friendship or relationship with someone that we allowed to wear us down emotionally or physically. Please note the intentional wording: *someone that we* allowed *to wear us down.* Accusing someone of doing something *to* us is coming from a victim's point of view. The truth is that whether it's conscious or unconscious, we allow other people to treat us in certain ways. It's up to us to manage our relationships and energy wisely, the same way that we all want to manage our money well, whenever possible.

If you're intuitive, you probably have the challenge of being extra sensitive to the energy around you, even if you might not be aware of it. It's in your best interest to learn how to interpret the sights, sounds and experiences around you and manage them. We're not talking about being a control freak and trying to make everyone around you act a certain way. We're talking about assessing situations energetically and deciding whether you want to be in that situation or not.

By the end of this chapter, you will:

- Understand when your intuition kicks in during dating situations
- Have examples of the energetic costs of following and not following your intuition
- Know how to ask questions about your dating experience with your dominant form of intuition in mind

When Does Your Intuition Start?

Have you ever had a case of refrigerator blindness? You can't find something that you *know* is in there. Someone else looks into the fridge and finds it, voilà! There it was, right in front of your nose, hidden in plain view. Dating is like that too. There are things you can see before, during and after a date that are in plain view; you're just not looking in the right place. If you learn to tune into your intuition, you'll have a much better dating experience right from the start. We're not asking you to turn into an overly critical cynic, just notice what you see right from the start.

Getting Schooled by a College Professor: A Story from Maryellen

My predominant mode of intuition is clairaudient. I've learned that *listening* to what happens before my actual dates is huge in determining the enjoyability of the date.

This was my worst date ever! Here's a story where I didn't cut off the date when I should have (before it happened) because I wasn't listening to my intuition.

Someone had added me to his Favorites category on an online dating site. He didn't have a photo on his profile and was older than most of the men that I've dated—two immediate potential deal-breakers for me. And as if that wasn't enough, I rarely contacted a man first, and I did that too! His profile said that because of his job, he didn't want his photo on the Match site. However, if you asked for a photo, he'd send a link.

I was kind of bored and lonely and asked him for his photo. Paul sent a link to his professional photo. He wasn't attractive but he was a college professor and the idea of having an intellectual conversation was kind of fun and exciting to me. We talked on the phone about going out to lunch.

He asked me where I lived and I said: "Downtown Scottsdale."

Then he asked me what my favorite restaurant was: "Il Postino," I said.

He responded: "Il Postino is nowhere near Downtown Scottsdale!"

Me: "You didn't ask me what my favorite restaurant was in downtown Scottsdale!"

He seemed very annoyed that I didn't get the connection that he was trying to find some place close to my home to be accommodating. I wasn't answering the way I did to be uncooperative or difficult. I was taking the question at face value.

After some discussion, he recommended that we go to a

restaurant called Sunflower, which was next door to an independent bookstore that he thought I would like. That restaurant was not close to downtown Scottsdale but I didn't care. When I got to the restaurant and saw him, he looked much older than his photo. I was disappointed but decided to make the best of it. We ordered our sandwiches at the counter and took them on a tray to the table. It wasn't exactly my idea of a nice restaurant but it wasn't awful either.

During the date he was talking about how hard it was to meet people because he was a college professor and his students were all over the area. I didn't see that as a huge problem but he did. My thinking was, as long as he's not asking out his students, what's the problem? In case you're unaware of this, college professors can get terminated for having relationships with their students. I'm pretty sure this is confined to the period at which the student is enrolled in the college but don't quote me on that.

At any rate, he gave an example: "For instance, I couldn't ask someone out in this restaurant, as that would be reputationally detrimental." What the heck? *Reputationally detrimental? Why couldn't he just say it wouldn't be good?*

I should have known better but I asked: "Why?" I've learned over the years that starting a question with the word "Why" can be very confrontational and accusatory. And, we women are Why-aholics. We really do want to know and understand why men do and say the things they do. "What makes you say that?" Would have been a better way to phrase the question.

Anyway, Paul went on to explain that if he asked out someone who was in the restaurant, he would get a reputation as someone that was always looking to ask women out.

I just wasn't buying it and again, without thinking, asked, "What are you afraid of?" (You can take the girl out of Jersey but you can't take the Jersey out of the girl!) He insisted that he wasn't afraid of anything, he just had a reputation to protect. It wasn't as simple as I was making it.

I went on to explain that in my view of the world, there was only approaching a situation in a mode of love or fearfulness. He strongly disagreed, saying that my view was way too simplistic and it was way more complicated than I was making it.

"Maybe it isn't..." I said and kind of chuckled because I used to think that situations were a lot more complicated too. That kind of thinking often left me exhausted and fatigued.

We proceeded to eat our lunch and after a minute or two of silence he asked, "What just happened here?"

I was pretty stunned. I didn't know what he meant. He elaborated that he wanted to know what just happened in the conversation. I answered something about how we had a disagreement and moved on. The only thing is, he hadn't moved on and was totally insulted. He felt challenged and angry and kept saying, "I wouldn't do that to someone."

I honestly wasn't sure what he was talking about but it was obvious he was very angry.

The date went downhill from there. He started accusing me of purposefully giving him a bad time because of the way he looked and his age. He was about ten years older than me. In a way, he was right because it always feels a little deceptive when someone online presents a photo that is them, but as a younger, thinner version than what they are now.

He went on to lecture me that it could have been a nice date but I obviously didn't have good enough manners to make it turn out that way. We both got up about the same time, realizing that the date was over and started to leave. He asked me something about how long I had been divorced and implied that the reason I was still dating was that I was so rude.

I said, "See ya..." just as an expression because I didn't know what else to say.

He replied: "I don't think so!"

Wow, what a big energetic price to pay because I was bored and felt like going out! I would have been better off taking myself to Il Postino and people-watching or staying at home watching Netflix. Now, I get to remember that monumentally bad date for the rest of my life. While I forgive myself for whatever it is I could have done differently, and forgive him for his perspective, this was far from the desired outcome.

What did I know and when did I know it? When does your intuition start? Here's the deal: It never goes off! It's just that sometimes you pay attention to it and sometimes you don't! Now that you are aware of that fact, you'll have to take more responsibility for your choices.

Let's look back at what happened and the auditory cues that I ignored.

When I was on the phone with him and we were in the process of choosing the restaurant, I felt tired, like he was wearing me out making suggestions. He asked me very clearly what my favorite restaurant was and I answered. At that point, if he had said, "Great, let's go to Il Postino!" that would have been a good indicator. Instead, he made me wrong for not choosing a restaurant in Scottsdale.

Whenever you feel tired from a conversation, it's a big red flag. The bottom line is that I shouldn't have been surprised that the date didn't go well. Energetically and spiritually, we were very mismatched. A better plan than jumping into the first date would have been to talk on the phone a little longer and then use greater discernment before meeting in person. That minimizes the potential energetic loss. And, as I've come to learn the hard way, what I *hear* is a big factor in how the date is going to go.

The Cheesecake Factory Factor: A Story from Maryellen

One night, I went out to a Meetup Group for singles simply because I was bored and tired of sitting home alone. (I had a pattern, eh?) The event was at a bar inside of a restaurant. Everyone ordered food and drinks and was standing around talking. One guy in particular was making a lot of jokes and seemed very amusing. He wasn't attractive to me but his personality seemed to somehow compensate for that. At the end of the evening he very confidently asked for my number and said he'd like to take me out to dinner. I was impressed by his confidence so I gave him my business card.

Joel called me the next day in the evening and told me that he had tried to call me twice earlier in the day and that my voicemail didn't pick up. That was both strange and alarming. I use the same phone for my business and personal calls. If my clients can't reach me, that's bad news. We hung up from our call and I had my mom call me and told her I wasn't going to pick up so she could leave me a message. She left me a message no problem. Hmmmm, that's strange, Joel insisted there was something wrong with my voicemail and said I should check with my phone company. He was so insistent that I call the phone company. I remember thinking: *The phone company will ask me if I had someone else leave a message and I'd have to say "yes, it worked."* I remember thinking at the time: *It must just be him or his phone.* I didn't like the fact that he wouldn't drop the idea that I had to call the phone company. On one hand it seemed like nothing, on the other hand, it seemed like a message; but what was the message about?

Later on that evening we talked again and Joel asked me if I wanted to go out to dinner. I accepted and then he said: *Do you like the Cheesecake Factory?* Well, as it happens, I had just heard that the Cheesecake Factory came up on a list of one of the most fattening restaurants to eat at, and that wasn't about the cheesecake. Plus, I live in Scottsdale, where there are dozens of fabulous independent restaurants with unique and beautifully presented food in lovely settings.

I had recently come to the realization that I was eating out a lot and would agree to go wherever the other person wanted to go in order to be congenial. The awareness came to me that I'd rather go somewhere that had really good food vs. a chain restaurant, where the food tastes the same no matter what city, state or country you were in. Why risk gaining weight eating mediocre food?

I don't remember exactly what I said, but I got the point politely across that I didn't want to go to the Cheesecake Factory.

Joel was obviously disappointed and said, "Okay, where do you want to go?" I named a few places and he said very unenthusiastically, "Yeah, I guess we could go there." Then he said, "Well, why don't you think about it and give me a call back when you figure out where you want to go."

We hung up and now I was confused. I had just told him a few places that I wanted to go and he told me to call him when I figured out where I wanted to go. Now I didn't even want to go out with him but I didn't know why. Based on my earlier story, I've subsequently learned that communication challenges right up front are a big red flag. It doesn't mean one person is wrong and one is right. It means that there's an incongruity in the relationship that is revealing itself. It's the opposite of everything going smoothly and easily.

I called my brother Charlie and described the situation to him.

"Am I being unreasonable not wanting to go to the Cheesecake Factory?"

He always gives me great advice and here's what he told me. "You're a foodie and someone that is with you is going to have to accept that and appreciate that about you. If he doesn't, then he's not the guy for you."

He was right and I decided not to call back Joel. I was thinking that he wasn't going to call me and that the way he left the conversation was a brush off. Okay, lesson learned, no worries.

He called! My initial reaction was: *Oh crap, I didn't plan on having another conversation with him!* Now I was going to have to decide if I was going to honor my time and energy or cave and go out with him and/or go to the Cheesecake Factory. This was about so much more for me than what appeared on the surface. This was about me putting what I want on the back burner for someone else.

He started the conversation by asking if I had figured out where I wanted to go. I told him that I thought about dating and I realized that I wasn't in the frame of mind to go out. The truth was that I wasn't in the frame of mind to go out with him, but there was no need to be cruel about it.

He said something like. "Well, if you decide that you want to go out or change your mind, give me a call."

I think we both knew that we were not going to talk again but since we were on the phone, it wasn't too awkward. After we hung up, I felt relieved.

This is one of the first times that I cut off a relationship energetically before it even started. There was one part of me that felt like a total bitch for not even trying to get to know him. There was another part of me that felt a new level of empowerment. I was acting on information that I already knew and not using my energy in an unproductive way.

It can feel pretty uncomfortable to agree to something and then not follow through. Sometimes, we don't have all the information that we need when we say yes to something and then feel anxiety going forward. While it's better to think things through before you say yes, it's not a crime to change your mind and save yourself some energy.

Even if your dominant form of intuition isn't hearing (clairaudient), communication challenges up front are a big red flag. It is to your benefit to take a little longer to discern if you want to go out with someone by talking to them on the phone first.

And if you think *you* have a bad date story, here's an unforgettable one!
You. Can't. Make. This. Stuff. Up!

And You Think *You* Had a Bad Date? An Epic Story from Diana

Here's the second part of the story about Sam that you read about earlier.

I had had a long history of jumping into relationship after relationship with men who frankly were probably best left as amazing lovers than potential long-term partners. In my early to late twenties, like many women, I was led by physical attraction and chemistry rather than taking the time to assess how emotionally available and compatible they were with me beyond the bedroom. This often led to confusion, heartache and well, another predictable breakup.

I tried to make a relationship out of something that was mostly hormones and a need to escape from the parts of myself I didn't want to see. So, when I turned thirty, clock ticking, I decided to go 180 degrees in the opposite direction of what I was used to. I would actually take the time to get to know them, assess their personality and long-term potential based on a few key areas: Did they want to have kids? Were they financially stable? And finally, would they bore me? I know, I still had a long way to go, but it was progress.

One of the lucky men who fit this profile was Sam, the man that we mentioned at the beginning of this book. If you don't remember, Sam was a lanky, funny, tall man in his thirties who was gainfully employed, but who, my intuition had hinted at early on, could be missing something pretty important. This was more than confirmed by the equivalent of a spirit "smackdown" that would go down in the coming weeks, but I was stubborn and didn't want to admit defeat. It would be so much more comfortable to be able to say, "I'm *finally* settling down everyone! You can stop worrying about me. And I can stop feeling like a crazy woman who isn't sure she ever, God-forbid, wants to get married!"

To back up just a bit, Sam and I went out a few more times and during that time there was no kissing, nothing. He was paying so I assumed it was a date. He picked me up and took me home. He complimented what I was wearing. But I was confused — where was the *spark*?

On the fourth date, I decided that I would make the first move. I had to know once and for all if we had any chemistry. So, when he asked to give me a massage, I thought to myself: *Yes, finally we're getting somewhere.* After the massage (all of our clothes stayed on), I planted one on him. It. Was. Awkward. He kissed me like a grandma kisses a grandchild. A smooch. But it got weirder.

As I tried harder and harder, more tongue here, less there, thinking that maybe it had been a while and he just needed to relax, etc., I heard him humming. *Humming?* Was that my clairaudience or was it seriously happening? The tune he was humming under his breath as I pulled out all the stops to force at least one note-worthy kiss?

Lady Gaga's "Bad Romance"!

I couldn't believe what my super-highly tuned ears were hearing. And he did it unaware. *Twice!* The first time I ignored it. The second time I didn't know whether to laugh or slap him.

Now at this point, I went out of body and on autopilot. It was as if I were in a bad B movie observing the scene as an extra, cringing at what was to come next. Totally confused about what to do next I said: "So, how about we pull an Angel card for you?"

For anyone who doesn't know what that means: Oracle Cards are decks of cards that are used for intuitive readings like tarot cards. Some Oracle Card decks have angel themes on them.

He gave me a goofy sideways smile and nodded curiously. I was pissed and my ego was screaming but I shuffled the cards with such conviction because I didn't know what else to do! And of all forty-four cards in the deck, the one he pulled was:

CAUTION IS WARRANTED. THIS SITUATION AS IT STANDS IS NOT RIGHT FOR YOU.

If that wasn't a sign that I needed to stop seeing him as boyfriend/partner material, I don't know what was! Maybe if he hummed "Alejandro" by Lady Gaga, then at least I could say pretty confidently, "Okay, he's gay!" and then we'd have a good chuckle and he could tell me what he really thought of my outfit.

I wish I could say that at that point, I said something clever and brushed it off, but I was really angry. I felt deceived and in denial, two emotions that, well, only prolong the inevitable. My clairsentience was lighting up as my stomach felt like someone had literally balled up their fists and sucker punched me. My throat was hot and constricted. Both of these signs are indications that I needed to express and communicate something and this would help me make an educated decision.

So I asked him point blank, "Where is this going?"

He shuffled a lot and said, "I see you as a friend. Can we be friends? We have *so* much in common."

I thought to myself: *Yeah, we both like musicals, we both like Lady Gaga and apparently we're both fans of Angels. But we are not fans of kissing each other and you need to go now!*

We parted ways and I realized that I needed to have more faith in myself and in the Universe. There is a saying that one of my mentors, Colette Baron-Reid, shared. She said, "Rejection is the Goddess's protection." What she meant by that is that every seemingly failed experience in life is really the Universe's way of removing all that is holding you from what is truly meant for you. I understand her words now but at the time, my method of coping was to have a full-blown ego party. I ate chocolate, took my ass to Barnes and Noble, flipped through *He's Just Not that Into You* to torture myself and bought a new top and jewelry. And sometimes, we need that. And sometimes we need an awkward date or an uncomfortable silence to remind us of who we really are and that we're not crazy after all.

Reflections

Put a screening policy in place even if you're initially very excited about someone. If you're a good match, a day or so isn't going to matter if you decide to schedule a date. Have a phrase that you're comfortable with that you can decline a date comfortably. For instance: *Joe, I know that I said I'd go out but in taking some time to think about it, I'm not really in the frame of mind for dating. I hope that you understand. I don't want to waste your time but appreciate the offer.* Most men appreciate direct communication like this.

If you change your mind about a date that you've accepted, use the Golden Rule. Don't be a no-show; "That's so *not* Bombshell!" as our friend Gigi Belmonico would say. She means: *you got yourself into the situation, so figure out how to get out as gracefully as possible.*

Trust your body's initial impression — not your mind, not your "list" of top 100 must-have qualities or other people's opinions, including the guy's! Diana knew from the first date that her body said: "No kissing but he is interesting…" and then acted surprised when the actual kiss was a flat-liner. You can seem like a great match on paper, but our bodies *know*.

You can be attracted to someone's energy and not have

them as a romantic partner. In Diana's case, she felt physically ill around Sam and had no idea what was going on or if she would someday be expected to have a sexual/ physical relationship with him (definitely not partner material!). However, she felt fine and comfortable when they were talking about life, hanging out and when the pressure for intimacy was off. This was a clear sign that he was a friend, which is great as long as the feeling is mutual.

This one is important; get a highlighter: Put on your favorite outfit.
If he ever hums Lady Gaga while you kiss him, sorry to tell you, honey, but *he's just not that into you!* And if you have doubts, pull out your oracle cards, but you'd better be ready to hear the truth!

Chapter Affirmation: My intuition is always working.

Chapter 7
Trust and Surrender

Trust yourself. Create the kind of self that you will be happy
to live with all your life. Make the most of yourself by fanning
the tiny, inner sparks of possibility into flames of achievement.

—Golda Meir

Right now you may be wondering: *When am I going to meet
him? I'm tired of being alone.* Surrendering doesn't mean
giving up on your dream to find a wonderful life partner.
Surrendering means allowing Divine timing to take
place. Have you ever noticed that when you really want
something and then you get it, the journey automatically
doesn't feel as long as it was? You have to have faith that
the Universe is aligning with you to bring you what you
want.

By the end of this chapter, you will know:

- A powerful example of setting a strong intention
- The importance of divine timing and letting go
  of control
- How surrendering your attachment to the way
  something happens brings you into alignment

As you learn how to trust and follow your intuition, you
will attract different potential partners into your life that
are of a higher energetic frequency than your past partners.
As you fine-tune what it is that you want, you will attract
people and circumstances that match that energy.

When it comes to finding love, surrendering takes great

courage. It's about being clear about what you are asking for, then following the signs and internal nudges towards that. Finally you have to detach from how you think everything is supposed to happen. It's not like submitting your resume for a job and getting a response within a certain period of time. It's more like wanting to find your keys, only to find them on the kitchen table right after you gave up.

That's the way love works. You know what you want (your keys/your soul mate), you are clear on how you want to feel (secure/solid/confident) and after taking action if it feels forced, you stop and fully engage in your life. When you do what brings you pleasure and joy you become more attractive to everyone around you.

Clear Intentions, Forced Actions and Surrendering to an Outcome: A Story from Maryellen

Sean Stephenson is a public speaker the likes of whom you have never seen. I'm not exactly sure how I found out about him, but it was probably from his Dance Party Video on YouTube. Sean was born with osteogenesis imperfecta, a brittle bone syndrome. He's about three feet tall and uses a wheelchair to get around. He has a very distinct and appealing voice, literally and figuratively.

I really wanted to meet Sean. We both live in Scottsdale, so I figured I might hear him speak somewhere locally. I heard that he was speaking at a National Speaker's Association event a while ago. I called up the Speaker's Association and asked what time and day he was speaking and couldn't get any information. Somehow, they didn't know what event I was talking about. I sent Tweets and inquired on Facebook about his appearance and no one seemed to know anything about it. It was one of those things I found out about in passing and then couldn't remember where I saw the information. A couple of months later, I discovered that my friend Kim had gone to Sean's event. I hadn't thought to ask her about it, even though I knew that she had met him once. Kim was in a Scottsdale restaurant called Grassroots and she introduced herself to Sean there.

A couple of months passed and I saw a new TEDx video featuring Sean at Ironwood State Prison. The talk was called "The Prison of your Mind." That video blew me away! Imagine talking to incarcerated people and being able to give them hope for mental freedom regardless of their circumstances? Now, my *wanting* to meet Sean Stephenson became *I have to* meet Sean Stephenson.

I had plans to go out to Happy Hour with some friends the day after I saw the TEDx video. I suggested Grassroots because it is a fun place and I love the food. My hidden agenda was possibly meeting Sean there, which I did not tell anyone.

As it happened though, right before I left the house, I sent an email a client in Canada. He's interested in personal development and I thought he would like to see the TEDx video. I ended the message by saying: Sean lives in Scottsdale and I hope to meet him someday.

I am a stickler for being on time, but for some reason, on this night, I stopped to send the email even though we were a few minutes late to pick up a friend.

I imagined what I would do if I saw Sean roll into the restaurant. I imagined what I would do if he was already seated. I wanted to be respectful of him, not seem like a star-struck groupie or something!

We were at Grassroots a long time before we left to go to a movie. No Sean. *Oh well*, I thought, *not tonight, but there will be another opportunity.*

After the movie, we went to an ice cream store called Sweet Republic that has been featured on The Food Network. You simply must go there if you are in Scottsdale or Phoenix! It was about 10:40 p.m. when we got there. We were laughing and talking and joking around about who knows what. We sat down and all of a sudden, I *heard* Sean talking! At the exact moment that I looked to my left, someone two tables over slightly leaned back in her seat and there he was, about four feet away. I just couldn't believe my eyes!

I kind of froze, not knowing what to do next. I hadn't told anyone about my secret Grassroots hope so I was completely astonished. My friends encouraged me to introduce myself to him and I got a great photo too. I can honestly say it was a highlight of my life to meet Sean who is a beacon of pure joy and love. The only experience that I've ever had that was similar was meeting Ram Dass, who had an other-worldly quality about him.

Get to know Sean's work. His mission is to rid the world of insecurity and we all need that, especially from someone that walks his talk!

Can you see how in the beginning I tried hard to meet Sean and couldn't get the information I needed? Then, I went from *wanting* to meet him to feeling like I *had* to meet him. After that, I contrived a situation to meet him at Grassroots, which didn't work. I *was* very attached to *how* I was going to meet him. Then, I just surrendered: *Oh well, not tonight.* And, since I'm primarily clairaudient, I heard him before I saw him! You can chalk the whole thing up to coincidence but Scottsdale is actually a large town and I'm not usually going out for ice cream at 10:30 p.m.! It was a great example of energetic alignment. That's what we've been teaching you in this book, aligning yourself to be a match with what you want.

Chapter Affirmation: The more I trust my intuition, the stronger my intuition gets.

Conclusion

If you've made it this far, congratulations!

We've taken an amazing journey together and just to re-cap what you've learned, you now know how to trust your intuitive channel or Clairs before and after a date, which will save you so much time and energy!

You know what to look for when it comes to online dating to make the experience worth your while.

You will have taken serious inventory of your space and let go of any old relationship baggage that is keeping you from calling in your new love.

You've forgiven yourself and those who hurt you.

You can stop going at it alone and know exactly how to call on two major archangels to help you heal your heart and get rid of ex energy.

You're clear on your relationship deal breakers so you will stop setting yourself up for heartbreak and start attracting people who want what you want. Yes, they *are* out there!

The biggest lesson of all is this: when you trust your intuition, you are back in the driver's seat of your life. You don't have to be a slave to your past disappointments because they got you this far, girlfriend! You can make new choices based on what's true for you now. And the future is bright when you trust yourself!

Your next step is to open your heart up to possibility. A possibility that you have everything you need to draw in the love that you are seeking. Remember this: What you

truly desire also desires you.
Believe. Believe. Believe.

No matter where you are in life or what happened before, love is possible. It's already within you. Our intuition told us so.

Chapter Affirmation: Every day, my intuition gets clearer and easier to understand quickly.

Next Steps

To stay connected with us and get more information on using your intuition in your relationships go here:

www.thedatingmirror.com

Get your
FREE
Bonus Gifts
at the link below!

http://www.thedatingmirror.com/bonusgifts

 https://www.facebook.com/thedatingmirror/

 @TheDatingMirror

About the Authors

Diana Dorell is a gifted intuitive and healer. She is a third-generation medicine woman who is passionate about helping you trust your intuition and release blocks to having a loving, healthy soulmate relationship, starting with yourself. She is a certified Angel Therapy Practitioner™ with Doreen Virtue, PhD, and holds a degree from Northwestern University.

What sets Diana apart from others in her field is her ability to quickly transform Divine messages into easily understandable, practical advice. Her joyful, gentle demeanor allows people to understand *exactly* what will help them most at *exactly* the right time. She has been a popular radio show host, public speaker and blogger on many media outlets including the State of Now #140 conference in New York City, KCTV Channel 5, SoulsJourney Radio, Achieve Radio and BlogTalkRadio to name a few. When she's not busy helping people connect with their Angels, she can be found dancing with children, Feng-Shuing her home and eating hazelnut Nutella gelato.

For information and free resources from Diana, please visit her website at http://www.DianaDorell.com

Maryellen Smith is *The Reinvention Queen*, and has been a writer since she was five years old. She is an expert at embracing change and through her own transformational journey has inspired others to tap into their intuitive power

and live authentic lives. She loves social media and is the proud owner of ReinventionQueen.com, a company that specializes in marketing and small business branding. She helps business owners bridge the gap between technology and marketing and assists them in expressing themselves in a creative and heart-centered way. She holds a master's degree in Technical Communication from North Carolina State University. At present, she calls Scottsdale, Arizona, home and when she's not busy writing or reinventing her world, she can be found cooking or taking photos of gourmet food and creating mermaid art in her living room.

To contact Maryellen, please visit her website at
http://www.ReinventionQueen.com

To work with Diana or Maryellen individually, please contact them via their websites.

66314203R00079

Made in the USA
Charleston, SC
14 January 2017